CORS Essentials

Cross Origin Resource Sharing

Rajesh Gunasundaram

Randall Goya

BIRMINGHAM - MUMBAI

CORS Essentials

First published: May 2017

Production reference: 1220517

Published by Packt Publishing Ltd.
Livery Place
35 Livery Street
Birmingham B3 2PB, UK.

ISBN 978-1-78439-377-9

www.packtpub.com

Credits

Authors
Rajesh Gunasundaram
Randall Goya

Commissioning Editor
Wilson D'souza

Acquisition Editor
Tushar Gupta

Content Development Editor
Aishwarya Pandere

Technical Editor
Dharmendra Yadav

Copy Editor
Manisha Sinha

Project Coordinator
Nidhi Joshi

Proofreader
Safis Editing

Indexer
Mariammal Chettiyar

Graphics
Tania Dutta

Production Coordinator
Shraddha Falebhai

Cover Work
Shraddha Falebhai

About the Authors

Rajesh Gunasundaram is a software architect, technical writer, and blogger. He has over 15 years of experience in the IT industry, with more than 10 years using Microsoft .NET, 2 years of BizTalk Server, and a year of iOS application development.

Rajesh is a founder and editor of technical blogs and , where you can find many of his technical writings on .NET and iOS.

Rajesh is also the founder and developer of a web product, a platform that analyses YouTube videos and channels.

Rajesh has also written a book *ASP.NET Web API Security Essentials*, for Packt Publishing.

Rajesh holds a masters degree in Computer Application and began his career as a software engineer in 2002. He worked on client premises located in various countries, such as the UK, Belarus, and Norway. He also has experience in developing mobile applications for iPhone and iPad.

His technical strengths include Azure, Xamarin, ASP.NET MVC, Web API, WCF, .NET Framework/.NET Core, C#, Objective-C, Angular, BizTalk, SQL Server, REST, SOA, design patterns, and software architecture.

Randall Goya has been a Senior Web Developer and Application Architect for enterprise organizations for several years, mostly specializing as a Drupal Consultant. Drupal as a framework is integrated with so many other applications and APIs, including payment gateways, media (Brightcove, YouTube, mp3, and video players), messaging (Amazon SQS, Mulesoft), as a content repository for other frameworks (WordPress), and for native mobile applications, and VOIP.

www.PacktPub.com

eBooks, discount offers, and more

Did you know that Packt offers eBook versions of every book published, with PDF and ePub files available? You can upgrade to the eBook version at and as a print book customer, you are entitled to a discount on the eBook copy. Get in touch with us at customercare@packtpub.com for more details.

At , you can also read a collection of free technical articles, sign up for a range of free newsletters and receive exclusive discounts and offers on Packt books and eBooks.

Get the most in-demand software skills with Mapt. Mapt gives you full access to all Packt books and video courses, as well as industry-leading tools to help you plan your personal development and advance your career.

Why subscribe?

- Fully searchable across every book published by Packt
- Copy and paste, print, and bookmark content
- On demand and accessible via a web browser

Customer Feedback

Thanks for purchasing this Packt book. At Packt, quality is at the heart of our editorial process. To help us improve, please leave us an honest review on this book's Amazon page at

If you'd like to join our team of regular reviewers, you can e-mail us at customerreviews@packtpub.com. We award our regular reviewers with free eBooks and videos in exchange for their valuable feedback. Help us be relentless in improving our products!

Table of Contents

Preface

This book will explain how to use CORS, including specific implementations for platforms such as Drupal, WordPress, IIS server, ASP.NET, JBoss, Windows Azure, and Salesforce, as well as how to use CORS in the Cloud on Amazon AWS, YouTube, Mulesoft, and others. It will examine the limitations, security risks, and alternatives to CORS. It will examine the W3C specification and major developer documentation sources about CORS. It will predict what kind of extensions to the CORS specification, or completely new techniques, may come in the future to address the limitations of CORS.

What this book covers

Chapter 1, *Why You Need CORS*, discusses the same-origin policy, which limits sharing resources across domains; granting access to CORS requests by setting headers; different ways to add more security; understanding preflight requests to prepare for some types of CORS methods and events; and alternatives to CORS.

Chapter 2, *Creating Proxies for CORS*, discusses what a Proxy Server is and various reasons to use a Proxy, different types of Proxy Servers, and reverse proxis in Node. js with CORS anywhere.

Chapter 3, *Usability and Security*, discusses CORS and XDomainRequest, detecting AJAX support in the browser, using preflight to ensure usability and improve security, handling access-control-allow-origin header with and without the wildcard, HTTP request and response headers for usability and security, CORS requests with credentials, and setting and reading cookies, and CORS security cheat sheet by OWASP.

Chapter 4, CORS in Popular Content Management Frameworks, discusses how to enable CORS in WordPress, Drupal, Joomla!, and Adobe Experience Manager (AEM).

Chapter 5, CORS in Windows, discusses implementing CORS on the Windows platform. The Windows platform includes IIS, ASP.NET Web API applications, and Windows Communication Foundation.

Chapter 6, CORS in the Cloud, discusses using CORS in cloud computing services such as Amazon Simple Storage Service (S3), Google Cloud Storage, IBM Cloudant, Windows Azure Storage, the Box.com API, and the Dropbox API.

Chapter 7, CORS in Node.js, discusses the Node.js platform and using CORS in JavaScript frameworks such as ReactJS, Ember.js, and Socket.IO, with examples based on the fundamentals of CORS with allowed origin(s), methods, and headers.

Chapter 8, CORS Best Practices, discusses best practices in enabling API-to-public CORS requests, limiting the API to allow CORS requests to a whitelisted set of origins, protecting against cross-site request forgery (CSRF), and minimizing preflight requests.

What you need for this book

- Any good JavaScript editor
- Wamp, Lamp, or Xamp, depending on the devlopment platform environment
- IIS to host the ASP.NET application
- Visual Studio 2012 or later to develop the ASP.NET Web API

Who this book is for

This book is intended for any web developer who works on various web applications with different technologies, developers who create APIs for external applications to consume, and developers who ensure security when cross-origin resource sharing happens.

Conventions

In this book, you will find a number of text styles that distinguish between different kinds of information. Here are some examples of these styles and an explanation of their meaning.

Code words in text, database table names, folder names, filenames, file extensions, path names, dummy URLs, user input, and Twitter handles are shown as follows: "Media files with the `<video>` and `<audio>` tags as long as the file type matches expected media formats."

A block of code is set as follows:

```
public static class WebApiConfig
{
  public static void Register(HttpConfiguration config)
  {
    // Other configurations omitted config.EnableCors();
    config.SetCorsPolicyProviderFactory(
      new DynamicPolicyProviderFactory());
  }
}
```

Any command-line input or output is written as follows:

```
PM> Install-Package Microsoft.AspNet.WebApi.Cors
```

New terms and **important words** are shown in bold. Words that you see on the screen, for example, in menus or dialog boxes, appear in the text like this: "Clicking the **Next** button moves you to the next screen".

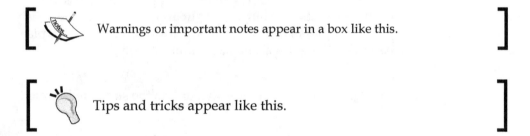

> Warnings or important notes appear in a box like this.

> Tips and tricks appear like this.

Reader feedback

Feedback from our readers is always welcome. Let us know what you think about this book—what you liked or disliked. Reader feedback is important for us as it helps us develop titles that you will really get the most out of.

To send us general feedback, simply e-mail feedback@packtpub.com, and mention the books title in the subject of your message.

If there is a topic that you have expertise in and you are interested in either writing or contributing to a book, see our author guide at www.packtpub.com/authors.

Customer support

Now that you are the proud owner of a Packt book, we have a number of things to help you to get the most from your purchase.

Errata

Although we have taken every care to ensure the accuracy of our content, mistakes do happen. If you find a mistake in one of our books—maybe a mistake in the text or the code—we would be grateful if you could report this to us. By doing so, you can save other readers from frustration and help us improve subsequent versions of this book. If you find any errata, please report them by visiting , selecting your book, clicking on the **Errata Submission Form** link, and entering the details of your errata. Once your errata are verified, your submission will be accepted and the errata will be uploaded to our website or added to any list of existing errata under the Errata section of that title.

To view the previously submitted errata, go to and enter the name of the book in the search field. The required information will appear under the **Errata** section.

Piracy

Piracy of copyrighted material on the Internet is an ongoing problem across all media. At Packt, we take the protection of our copyright and licenses very seriously. If you come across any illegal copies of our works in any form on the Internet, please provide us with the location address or website name immediately so that we can pursue a remedy.

Please contact us at copyright@packtpub.com with a link to the suspected pirated material.

We appreciate your help in protecting our authors and our ability to bring you valuable content.

Questions

If you have a problem with any aspect of this book, you can contact us at questions@packtpub.com, and we will do our best to address the problem.

1
Why You Need CORS

In this chapter, you will learn about the following:

- The same-origin policy that limits sharing resources across domains
- Granting access to CORS requests by setting headers
- How to do something with the `responseText` request from a CORS request
- Rudimentary security in CORS and ways to add more security
- Preflight requests to prepare for some types of CORS methods and events
- Enabling the crossorigin attribute in a script tag for better troubleshooting
- Alternatives to CORS: JSON-P, WebSockets, and window.postMessage

The same-origin policy

Sooner or later, web developers run up against the same-origin policy. Maybe you want to trigger a script on one domain and use the results on a different domain, but you can't.

The same-origin policy is necessary for web application security. The execution of a script may expose sensitive information. Access to this information is limited to the same domain where the script is located, unless access for an external domain has been specifically allowed by code.

 The same-origin policy is defined by the Internet Engineering Task Force (IETF) (`https://tools.ietf.org/html/rfc6454#page-4`).

A major motivation for implementing the same-origin policy is to protect sensitive information stored in **cookies** from being exposed to another domain. Web applications maintain authenticated user sessions in cookies. The user's personalizations and account information are stored in cookies. To ensure data confidentiality, cookies may not be shared across domains. For cookies, the same origin is shared by the domain or a sub-domain of that domain. For DOM elements such as scripts, the restrictions are more fine-grained.

The same-origin policy also applies to requests made with **XMLHttpRequest** (**XHR**). We will see how the **Access-Control-Allow-Origin** header facilitates the bending of the same-origin policy.

Notably, JSON-P, WebSocket, and window.postMessage are not restricted by the same-origin policy.

Considering the origin of entities

Access to DOM elements is allowed only when the request scheme, hostname, and port number match those of the current URI. A subdomain cannot share DOM elements with the parent domain.

- **Scheme** in web applications is typically `http://` or `https://`
- **Hostname** is typically the domain name plus TLD, or the unique IP address
- **Port number:**
  - Typically, port `80` is implicit in `http://`
  - `443` for SSL over `https://`

If the Scheme, Hostname, and port number do not match the DOM element, then resource sharing is prohibited as they do not share the same origin. Considering the domain `http://www.example.com`, the following table provides various combinations of matching and mismatching origins:

URI	Match?	Reason
`http://www.example.com/dir1/page1.html`	Match	Same protocol and host
`http://username:password@www.example.com/dir2/otherpage.html`	Match	Same protocol and host
`http://example.com/dir/page1.html`	Mismatch	Different host (www is a subdomain)
`https://www.example.com/dir/page1html`	Mismatch	Different protocol (`https://`)

URI	Match?	Reason
`http://www.example.com:81/dir/page1.html`	Mismatch	Same protocol and host but different port (`81`)
`http://en.example.com/dir/page1.html`	Mismatch	Different host (en is a subdomain)

Internet Explorer exception policy

Internet Explorer (IE) implements two major differences when it comes to the same-origin policy:

- **IE Trust Zones allow different domains**: If both domains are in a highly trusted zone, then the same-origin policy limitations are not applied.

- **Port is ignored**: IE ignores the port in same origin components. These URIs are considered from the same origin:

    - `http://www.example.com:80/dir/page1.html`

    - `http://www.example.com:81/dir/page1.html`

 These exceptions in Internet Explorer are non-standard and are not supported in other browsers. If an application is only viewed in Windows RT mobile or Internet Explorer, then these exceptions could be useful.

Commonly allowed cross-origin resource sharing

The same-origin policy is not required for many resources that may be embedded in cross-origin. The sharing of specific file types is limited by file type headers and ensuring that the file extensions and file meta data match the expected type.

DOM elements allowed for cross-origin sharing

The following information box displays scenarios where DOM elements are allowed for cross-origin sharing:

Images with the `<img>` tag, as long as the file type matches expected image formats.

Media files with the `<video>` and `<audio>` tags as long as the file type matches expected media formats.

JavaScript with the `<script src="..."></script>` tag. This method is used by many third-party applications, which embed a script to act upon the local resources, for example, a social media sharing service that analyzes the shareable images and other assets on current page and reads the URI.

CSS with the `<link rel="stylesheet" href="...">` tag. Cross-origin CSS requires a correct content-type header. Client.

Plugins with the `<applet>`, `<object>` and `<embed>` tags.

Fonts with `@font-face`. Support for this method varies by client browser.

Any content or URI loaded with the `<frame>` and `<iframe>` tags.

The X-Frame-Options header can prevent interaction between frames on different domains.

Allowing cross-origin sharing in WebSockets

The ability of WebSockets to bypass the same-origin policy is seen as a security risk. Using WebSockets on a gateway/server that supports origin-based security provides header-based security similar to CORS.

Limited cross-origin JavaScript API access

JavaScript APIs, such as iframe.contentWindow, window.parent, window.open, and window.opener, provide limited cross-origin access to the Window and Location objects. Some browsers permit access to more properties than the specification allows. You can use window.postMessage instead to communicate between documents in separate windows.

Permissions required by JavaScript

Let's consider content scraping. You can write a content scraping script that reads the rendered DOM of an external URI and creates local DOM elements with the same content, without any special configurations.

But what if you first need to run a script on the external URI, for example, to find out whether the user is the same as on your local site? You cannot trigger that external script and return the results without cross-origin sharing via CORS or a similar method to get around the same-origin policy.

JavaScript data storage access is strictly limited by origin

JavaScript data stored in the browser as Local Storage, or in IndexedDB, is separated by origin. Each origin has distinct storage, and JavaScript in one origin cannot read from or written to storage belonging to another origin unless it is given explicit access to a script on another domain by CORS or a similar method.

How CORS works – the header and the request

CORS is a specification of **World Wide Web Consortium (W3C)** http://www.w3.org/TR/cors/.

Cross Origin Resource Sharing (CORS) is allowed by having a header on the target domain where your local domain needs access. Local domains whitelisted in the allow-origin header can now send an **XMLHttpRequest (XHR)** request or other types of request to the target domain and receive a response.

Local domain and target domain explained

In this book, we will refer to the domains in a CORS request as follows:

- Local domain (`localdomain.com`): The domain making the CORS request
- Target domain (`targetdomain.com`): The domain receiving the CORS request, hence the target of the request

The CORS header

The CORS header whitelists access to one domain or any domain with the wildcard `*`. This header allows access from only one domain — the one specified:

```
Access-Control-Allow-Origin: http://localdomain.com
```

To enable access from multiple domains, a wild card is used:

```
Access-Control-Allow-Origin: *
```

Not being able to whitelist a list of allowed domains is a major complaint about CORS. Although a list of allowed domains is part of the W3C specification, in practical terms, it is not supported by browsers. (`http://www.w3.org/TR/cors/#list-of-origins`)

You can specify a single allowed domain or allow from all. The wildcard opens the target site to possible security risks because any domain is allowed to send a cross-origin request to the target domain.

Some authentication/authorization must be added outside of the CORS code to provide security, particularly when using the wildcard.

Example 1 – CORS request with JavaScript

The following example explains the CORS syntax, without actually doing anything with the `responseText` request:

- Create the `XMLHttpRequest` object:

```
// Create the XHR object.
function createCORSRequest(method, url) {
  var xhr = new XMLHttpRequest();
  if ("withCredentials" in xhr) {
    // XHR for Chrome/Firefox/Opera/Safari and IE >= 10
    xhr.open(method, url, true);
  } else if (typeof XDomainRequest != "undefined") {
```

```
    // XDomainRequest for IE <= 9
    xhr = new XDomainRequest();
    xhr.open(method, url);
  } else {
    // CORS not supported
    xhr = null;
  }
  return xhr;
}
```

- The `createCORSRequest` function does the following:

    1. Defines the new `XMLHttpRequest` request as the variable `"xhr"`.

    2. Checks whether the browser supports CORS via `XHR` by detecting the `withCredentials` or `XDomainRequest` properties.

    3. Opens the request for a resource on the target domain.

- These are the parameters passed to `createCORSRequest(method, url)`:

    ○ The method would typically be `GET`, `POST`, or another method

    ○ The URL is the URI of the resource requested by the local domain

IE 10 supports the working draft `XMLHttpRequest` level 2. Therefore, the `withCredentials` property can be used to detect CORS support in most browsers, including IE >= 10. To provide backwards compatibility for IE < 10, use its `XDomainRequest` property.

 Microsoft Internet Explorer 9 makes up 9.14% of desktop browsers, so we must include a fallback check for its the `XDomainRequest` property when `withCredentials` fails.

Passing a request to a utility function

```
var request = createCORSRequest("get", "targetdomain.com/");
if (request){
    request.onload = function(){
        //do something with request.responseText
    };
    request.send();
}
```

This request does two things:

- If `createCORSRequest()` returns an `XHR` object, it sends the request
- When the XHR ready state is loaded--request.onload--do something with `request.responseText`

Example 2: the CORS transaction to retrieve the title tag

This CORS request retrieves the page title from the target domain, `targetdomain.com`. It parses the `responseText` request to get the title and sends the target domain and the retrieved page title text to the `console.log`:

```
// Create the XHR object.
function createCORSRequest(method, url) {
  var xhr = new XMLHttpRequest();
  if ("withCredentials" in xhr) {
    // XHR for Chrome/Firefox/Opera/Safari and IE >= 10
    xhr.open(method, url, true);
  } else if (typeof XDomainRequest != "undefined") {
    // XDomainRequest for IE <= 9
    xhr = new XDomainRequest();
    xhr.open(method, url);
  } else {
    // CORS not supported
    xhr = null;
  }
  return xhr;
}

// utility function to parse the title tag from the response
function getTitle(text) {
  return text.match('<title>(.*)?</title>')[1];
}

// Make the actual CORS request
function makeCorsRequest() {
// we want the title of the page at targetdomain.com
  var url = 'targetdomain.com';
// use the GET method to return the entire page
  var xhr = createCORSRequest('GET', url);
  if (!xhr) {
    // log message if CORS is not supported
```

```
        console.log('CORS not supported');
        return;
    }
    // Response handlers.
    // on readyState = load
    xhr.onload = function() {
        // xhr.responseText contains the HTML for the page at
    targetdomain.com
        var text = xhr.responseText;
        // send the responseText to the utility function to extract the
    page title
        var title = getTitle(text);
        // do something with the processed responseText, in this case log
    a message
        console.log('response from request to ' + url + ': ' + title);
    };

    // error handler
    xhr.onerror = function() {
        console.log('error making the request');
    };

    // send the request
    xhr.send();
}
```

What happens in this CORS request?

1. The `XMLHttpRequest` request is created with the detection of CORS and error handling.

2. The `responseText` request returns the contents of the page at `targetdomain.com` with `GET`.

3. The `getTitle` function is executed on the `responseText` request, and it returns the title text.

4. The target domain URL and the title text are sent to the `console.log`.

You're probably thinking, "Big deal! I can get the title text in other ways.". But you could do more than retrieving a DOM element.

Distributing DOM elements to multiple domains

Let's consider a scenario in which you want to distribute a block-level DOM element, for example, a navigation menu from a target domain to multiple pages on multiple domains, along with customized CSS and JavaScript for the menu. You only change the navigation menu once on the target domain and copy it to multiple pages on multiple domains with CORS.

We will examine the pieces and then put them all together.

A `script` tag on the local domain embeds a script from the target domain. The same origin policy allows `script` tags to request resources across domains. The CORS script on the target domain will contain the `createCORSRequest` function and a request like this:

```
var request = createCORSRequest("GET", "targetdomain.com/header.php");
```

The CORS request allows you to GET a PHP file from the target domain and use it on the local domain.

You are not limited to requesting the HTML for a page on the target domain in the `responseText` request, as in example 2; `header.php` on the target domain may contain HTML, CSS, JavaScript, and any other code that is allowed in a PHP file.

 We are only reading `header.php`. Its contents are created by a process on the target domain outside of CORS. A script on the target domain scrapes the navigation menu and adds the necessary CSS and JavaScript. This script may be run as a Cron job to automatically update `header.php`, and it can also be triggered manually by an administrator on the target domain.

If the request is successful, it returns the contents of header.php and replaces the contents of a DOM element #global-header on the local domain with the responseText request:

```
if (xhr){
  xhr.onload = function(){
    // do stuff if request is successful;
  document.getElementById('#global-header').innerHTML =        xhr.
responseText ;
  };
 request.send();
}
```

Adding the `Access-Control-Allow-Origin` header in `header.php` on the target domain allows access from the local domain. Since `header.php` is a PHP file, we add the header with the PHP code. Use the wildcard * to allow access from any domain because we making the CORS request from multiple domains:

```php
<?php
header('Access-Control-Allow-Origin: *');
?>
```

You can place the CORS request script on the target domain as `cors_script.js` and trigger it with the script tag on your local domain. The `responseText` request is sent to any local domain page that contains the script tag. The DOM selector #global-header is replaced on the local domain with the `responseText` request contents of `header.php`, which contains the navigation menu HTML, CSS, and JavaScript from the target domain. We are also going to replace the logo image on the local domain with the one from the target domain.

By placing a script tag on your local domain page, you can access a target domain from any local domain, run a script on it, and do something on your local domain:

```
<script src="http://targetdomain.com/cors_script.js"></script>
```

Putting it all together

The contents of `cors_script.js` in the target domain are as follows:

```js
// Create the XHR object.
function createCORSRequest(method, url) {
  var xhr = new XMLHttpRequest();
  if ("withCredentials" in xhr) {
    // XHR for Chrome/Firefox/Opera/Safari and IE >= 10
    xhr.open(method, url, true);
  } else if (typeof XDomainRequest != "undefined") {
    // XDomainRequest for IE <= 9
    xhr = new XDomainRequest();
    xhr.open(method, url);
  } else {
    // CORS not supported
    xhr = null;
  }
  return xhr;
}

// set some variable values for use in the request processing
// the Target Domain  is contained in document.domain
```

```
var rawdomain = document.domain;
// add the http:// scheme
var sourceURL = "//" + rawdomain; // use the Protocol-relative
shorthand //

// define XHR request
var request = createCORSRequest("get", sourceURL + "/[path-to-file]/
header.php");

// send the request and process it if it is successful
if (request){
  request.onload = function(){
    // do stuff if CORS request is successful and loads
    // if it fails, there is no replacement of existing HTML in target
site
    // replace contents of #global-header on Local Domain with the
responseText
    document.getElementById('global-header').innerHTML = request.
responseText;
    // use logo image from Target Domain inside #branding container
 on Local Domain
    document.getElementById('branding').getElementsByTagName('img')
[0].src = sourceURL + '[path-to-logo]/targetdomain_logo.png';
  };
  request.send();
}
```

The navigation menu is automatically distributed to any number of pages on any number of domains via CORS whenever a page with the script tag loads.

Securing when all domains are whitelisted

What happens if someone copies your script tag to some other domain where the script was not intended to run? Since we whitelisted access from any domain with **Access-Control-Allow-Origin**: *, the request will be allowed from any domain; if the page also has the matching DOM selector #global-header, the script will copy the content from the target domain to the page making the request.

Although the W3C specification for CORS recommends providing a list of allowed origins, in practice, this is not widely implemented in browsers.

Ways to add security when a CORS header whitelists all domains

Techniques have been proposed to first match `$_SERVER['HTTP_ORIGIN']` to an allowed list, then write the header that allows the matched origin. Since `$_SERVER['HTTP_ORIGIN']` is not reliable, or the requesting domain may be served via a CDN that does not match the expected domain, this technique may not work.

An alternative method is to add allowed domains in `.htaccess` or in the server conf, which may have the same trouble with CDN domains.

Methods to add security when a CORS header whitelists all domains

There are a few methods to secure when all the domains are whitelisted in the CORS header. The following code compares the `HTTP_ORIGIN` with a list of allowed domains; if it matches, then the CORS header is written using the matched domain:

```
$http_origin = $_SERVER['HTTP_ORIGIN'];
if ($http_origin == "http://domain1.com" || $http_origin == "http://
domain2.com" || $http_origin == "http://domain3.info")
{
    header("Access-Control-Allow-Origin: $http_origin");
}
```

This technique may not work because `$_SERVER['HTTP_ORIGIN']` is not reliable, or the requesting domain may be served via a CDN that does not match the expected domain.

An alternative method is to add allowed domains in `.htaccess` or in the server conf, which may have the same trouble with CDN domains.

CORS headers can not provide reliable security

The CORS headers give browser information about allowed domains, but some other security policies, such as **cookies** or **OAuth**, can enforce tighter security in your application.

Simple CORS request methods

Most CORS request methods use either GET or POST, and less often HEAD. Keep these differences in mind when you are selecting the method to use:

- Browsers cache the result from a GET request; if the same GET request is made again, then the cached result will be returned. Repeating a GET request that has been cached will NOT return a response after the first request. If your code checks for a response, it will only be returned the first time.

- The POST method is typically used when you are updating information on the server. Repeating a POST method more than once may not return the same result. A POST will always obtain the response from the server. The content is sent separately from the headers in POST, which makes it more complicated than a simple GET request.

- The HEAD method is used to check resources, so only the headers are returned without any content. HEAD can check for the existence of a resource, its size, or to see whether it has been recently updated.

> GET, POST, and HEAD function in CORS exactly as they do for an XMLHttpRequest request.

CORS with Preflight

Preflight is a request the XHR object makes to ensure it's allowed to make another request.

> The CORS specification requires browsers to preflight requests that do the following:
> - Use any methods in the request other than GET, POST, or HEAD.
> - Include custom headers
> - Include content-type other than text/plain, application/x-www-form-urlencoded, or multipart/form-data

There's no preflight by default in CORS. Adding preflight makes your application more robust and handles errors better. However, it can also introduce complexities, which may be unnecessary when you are confident that the XHR request you need to make will be answered, and you only need to use GET, POST, or HEAD.

Triggering a preflight by setting a custom header

To trigger a preflight, set custom headers on the XHR request; the Access-Control-Allow-Methods header determines which HTTP methods can be used.

The preflight request

The following PHP code verifies for the OPTIONS request method during preflight. The server responds with the X-Requested-With header permitted:

```
if ($_SERVER['REQUEST_METHOD'] == 'OPTIONS') {
  // return only headers
  // The Preflight checks that the GET request method is supported
  if (isset($_SERVER['HTTP_ACCESS_CONTROL_REQUEST_METHOD']) && $_
SERVER['HTTP_ACCESS_CONTROL_REQUEST_METHOD'] == 'GET') {
    header('Access-Control-Allow-Origin: *');
    header('Access-Control-Allow-Headers: X-Requested-With');
  }
  exit;
}else{
  // error-handling code if the OPTIONS request method is unavailable
}
```

The preflight response

A successful server response returns the X-Requested-With method:

```
HTTP/1.1 200 OK
Access-Control-Allow-Origin: *
Access-Control-Allow-Headers: X-Requested-With
```

CORS via jQuery

CORS via jQuery does not use preflight.

jQuery specifically avoids setting the custom header when making a CORS request. Therefore, it is better to use a separate preflight method when using jQuery for CORS.

Here is the comment in the jQuery xhr.js library explaining why preflight is not used:

// X-Requested-With header

// For cross-domain requests, seeing as conditions for a preflight are

// akin to a jigsaw puzzle, we simply never set it to be sure.

// (it can always be set on a per-request basis or even using AJAXSetup)

// For same-domain requests, won't change header if already provided.

Known issues with CORS preflight

There are some common issues that developers face while implementing CORS preflight.

Preflight in Firefox

The CORS preflight request fails in Firefox when the OPTIONS request needs to be authenticated, causing the cross-origin request to fail. The request fails because authentication tokens are not sent with the preflight request. If the OPTIONS request fails, the preflight will result in 405 (method not allowed). Firefox ignores the request when the preflight fails.

Preflight in Chrome

Unlike Firefox, Chrome allows the request even if the option fails in preflight if the request and response headers are correct.

Preflight in Internet Explorer

Even when using withCredentials, IE doesn't send the auth tokens to preflight.

Should we avoid preflight entirely?

The best advice is to avoid using preflight entirely, unless you need to check whether requests are allowed.

Non-simple CORS request methods and headers require preflight

Any CORS request that uses a non-simple method or header requires preflight.

GET, POST, and HEAD are considered simple requests (and are case-sensitive). They do not require preflight.

The simple headers that do not require preflight are as follows:

- Cache-control
- Content-language
- Content-type
- Expires
- Last-modified
- Pragma

Any other method or header requires preflight.

Using the XMLHttpRequest level 2 event HandlersOriginally, XMLHttpRequest had only one event handler: onreadystatechange. XMLHttpRequest2 introduces new event handlers.

You may have noticed that when defining the XHR objects, we have used request. onload, which corresponds to the onload event when the request has successfully completed since we are interested in knowing whether the request has been successful.

Event handler	Description
Onreadystatechange	readyState property changes
onloadstart*	request starts
Onprogress	during loading and sending data.
onabort*	request has been aborted
Onerror	request has failed
Onload	request has successfully completed
ontimeout	specified timeout has expired before the request could complete
onloadend*	request has completed (success or failure)

* IE's XdomainRequest does not support handlers marked with asterisks

Checking for the withCredentials property

Check whether `withCredentials` property is available to determine whether the browser supports `XMLHttpRequest` level 2 event handlers. This could be handled as a preflight.

Troubleshooting and debugging CORS

Detecting problems with CORS requires enabling the crossorigin attribute in the `<script>` tag.

Normal script tags will pass the least information to window.onerror for scripts that do not pass the standard CORS checks. To allow error logging for sites that use a separate domain for static media, several browsers have enabled the `crossorigin` attribute for scripts using the same definition as the standard crossorigin attribute for the `<img>` tag.

Browser support for crossorigin attribute in the <script> tag

Browser	Chrome	Firefox (Gecko)	Internet Explorer	Opera	Safari
Crossorigin attribute support	Version >= 30.0	Version >= 13	Not supported	Version >= 12.50	(Yes)

CORS with jQuery

jQuery's `$.ajax()` method can be used for standard XHR and CORS requests.

Things to know about CORS with jQuery2

JQuery's CORS implementation doesn't support IE's `XDomainRequest` object, which is needed prior to Internet Explorer 10. There are jQuery plugins and `workarounds`. `$.support.cors` can signal support for CORS. It is set to true if the browser supports CORS (but in IE it always returns false). This can be a quick way to check for CORS support.

In jQuery, define the XHR functions using the same techniques as for CORS with JavaScript:

```
$.ajax({
  // The 'type' property sets the HTTP method
  // Any value other than GET, POST, HEAD (eg. PUT or DELETE methods)
will initiate a preflight request
  type: 'GET',

  // The Target Domain URL to make the request to
  url: 'http://targetdomain.com',

  // The 'contentType' property sets the 'Content-Type' header
  // The JQuery default for this property is
  // 'application/x-www-form-urlencoded; charset=UTF-8'
  // If you set this value to anything other than
  // application/x-www-form-urlencoded, multipart/form-data, or text/
plain,
  // you will trigger a preflight request
  contentType: 'text/plain',

    xhrFields: {
      // The 'xhrFields' property sets additional fields on the
XMLHttpRequest
      // This can be used to set the 'withCredentials' property
      // Set the value to 'true' to pass cookies to the server
      // If this is enabled, your server must respond with the header
      // 'Access-Control-Allow-Credentials: true'
      // Remember that IE <= 9 does not support the 'withCredentials'
property
      withCredentials: false
    },

    headers: {
      // Set custom headers
      // If you set any non-simple headers, your server response must
include
      // the headers in the 'Access-Control-Allow-Headers' response
header
    },

    success: function() {
      // Handler for a successful response, do something with the
response.Text
    },

    error: function() {
```

```
        // Error handler
        // Note that if the error was due to an issue with CORS,
        // this function will still be triggered, but there won't be any
    additional information about the error.
    }
});
```

jQuery CORS AJAX plugin

A jQuery plugin for CORS is available at `http://plugins.jquery.com/cors`.

The plugin sends cross-domain AJAX requests through `corsproxy.io`.

Chapter 2, Creating Proxies for CORS, gives details about using proxies with CORS.

Enabling CORS globally with server configuration

Depending on your web server, you may be able to add the `Access-Control-Allow-Origin` header to allow CORS globally on every page in the server configuration.

Enabling CORS globally is not recommended since it removes granular control per page or application.

 Enabling CORS globally may be useful when you are only running a single application on the server, and every page needs to support CORS. By adding the header in the server configuration, you do not need to add the `Access-Control-Allow-Origin` header on a per-page basis.

Alternatives to CORS

There are other ways to work around the same-origin policy. CORS provides better basic security, error handling, preflight, and other methods that make it a superior choice for cross-origin sharing compared to these alternatives

Alternative methods include the following:

- JSON-P
- WebSocket
- window.postMessage

JSON-PJSONP (later dubbed JSON-P, or JSON-with-padding) was proposed in 2005 as a way to use the `<script>` tag to request data in the JSON format across domains.

The term "padding" refers to a `callback` function, which is defined as a query parameter attached to the `<script>` tag. The `callback` function is defined on the target domain. The `<script>` tag on the local domain loads a function or service on the target domain. When the script executes, the function on the target domain is called, and the data returned from the target domain is passed to the `callback` function on the local domain.

There is no official definition or specification for JSON-P.

Example of JSON-P

1. A callback function is defined on the local domain:

```
function handle_data(data) {
    // something is done to the data received from the Target
Domain
}
```

2. A `<script>` tag on the local domain loads the script (`http://targetdomain/web/service`) from the target domain and passes the results to the `callback` function `handle_data` on the local domain:

```
<script type="application/javascript" src="http://targetdomain/web/service?callback=handle_data" </script>
```

Using JSON-P – limitations and risks

*   JSON-P does not use AJAX XHR; therefore, error detection and handling are not possible until the data is passed to the `callback` function.

*   Trust in the target domain is implicit. If the target domain is compromised, the local domain becomes vulnerable as well. JSON-P is subject to cross-site request forgery (CSRF or XSRF) attacks because the `<script>` tag is not restricted by the same-origin policy. A script tag on a malicious page can request and obtain JSON data of another domain. If the user is authenticated at the endpoint domain, passwords or other sensitive data may get compromised.

*   Rosetta flash uses adobe flash player to exploit servers with a vulnerable JSON-P endpoint. It causes the Adobe Flash Player to accept a flash applet as originating from the same domain.

Proposed JSON-P validation standard

The standard would make JSON-P safer.

- These recommendations are made on `http://www.json-p.org/`. Limit the function ("padding") reference of the JSON-P response to a single expression as a function reference or an object property function reference. A single pair of enclosing parentheses should follow the expression, with a valid and parsable JSON object inside the parentheses.

  Examples of safer JSON-P functions are as follows:

  `functionName({JSON});`

  `obj.functionName({JSON});`

  `obj["function-name"]({JSON});`

- Only whitespace or JavaScript comments may appear in the JSON-P response since whitespace and comments are ignored by the JavaScript parser. The MIME-type `application/json-p` and/or `text/json-p` must be included in the requesting `<script>` element. The browser can require that the response must match the MIME-type.

 However, MIME-type `application/json-p` and/or `text/json-p` are not supported by any browser. CORS is a safer and more robust method than JSON-P for sharing resources across domains with JavaScript.

WebSocket

WebSocket provides full-duplex communication channels over a single TCP connection. The WebSocket protocol was standardized by the IETF (`https://tools.ietf.org/html/rfc6455`) in 2011, and the WebSocket API is a candidate recommendation by the W3C (`http://www.w3.org/TR/websockets/`).

WebSocket uses TCP, not HTTP; nor does it use AJAX/XHR.

Socket.io provides a framework to use WebSocket by creating a node.js server for the socket (`http://socket.io/`).

WebSocket handshakes

The initial handshake over HTTP sets up the connection and communicates the origin policy information.

If the handshake is successful, the data transfer continues via TCP.

WebSocket creates a two-way communication channel, where each side can, independently from the other, send data at will.

WebSocket and cross-domain resource sharing

A cross-domain WebSocket is enabled with the domain (host) header to accept/deny requests.

Risks of using WebSocket for cross-domain resource sharing

* The header can be spoofed. In order to secure the connection, you will need to authenticate the connection by other means.

* The same-origin policy is not observed in WebSocket; therefore, **Cross-Site WebSocket Hijacking (CSWSH)** is possible.

* WebSocket does not handle standard safeguards that need to be implemented outside of the WebSocket:

  ◦ Authentication
  ◦ Authorization
  ◦ Sanitization of data

The window.postMessage method

The postMessage method is part of the W3c candidate recommendation for HTML5 Web Messaging ().

postMessage allows messages between discrete documents. The documents may include an iframe embedded in a document, or any other window objects.

The postMessage method dispatches MessageEvent in the target window when a script is completed.

postMessage risks and security measures

- Any window can send a message to any other window. An unknown sender can send malicious messages. The sender's identity can be verified using the origin and source properties. If a site you trusted gets compromised, it can send cross-site scripting messages. The syntax of the received message can be verified against an expected pattern.

- A malicious script can spoof the `location` property of the window and intercept data. Similar to avoiding the wildcard in the `Access-Control-Allow-Origin` header in CORS, specify an exact target.

> The obvious security measure is not to use `postMessage` and not to add any event listeners for message events if you don't expect to receive messages.

Summary

We looked at the same-origin policy, which limits cross-origin resource sharing. We covered a lot of the basics needed to work around the same-origin policy with CORS, including the header and request.

We saw how a script tag on a local domain can retrieve resources from a target domain as `responseText` request and how we can then do things with the `responseText` request on the local domain.

We have learned when preflight is helpful, and when it is required.

We have learned how to enable the crossorigin attribute in the script tag for troubleshooting.

We have looked at CORS with jQuery and its limitations.

We have compared CORS with other cross-origin methods: JSON-P, WebSockets, and window.postMessage. We have learned why CORS can be better and more secure than these methods.

In the next chapter, we will learn how to use proxies for CORS, for example, using the CORS plugin for jQuery with corsproxy.io.

2
Creating Proxies for CORS

A proxy generally acts as an agent or an intermediary for a client that requests for a resource from a server. In this chapter, we will learn about the following:

- What is a proxy server?
- Reasons to use a proxy server
- Types of proxy server: forward and reverse proxies
- Reverse proxy in node.js with CORS anywhere

Proxies and the World Wide Web

Generally speaking, a proxy is someone or something that has the authority to represent some other person or thing; for example, a proxy may be authorized to vote on behalf of another person.

The World Wide Web is composed of individual machines communicating with each other. A web proxy acts as an intermediary with the authority to communicate with a third-party server on behalf of a server contacting the proxy server. Modern web applications are often distributed across many servers, and proxies can tie them together.

What is a proxy server?

A proxy server handles requests from clients asking for resources from another server. The requests may be for resources, such as files, web pages, or other resources from different servers. If the request is validated, the proxy server retrieves the resource and sends it to the requesting client. There are many types of proxy; they share the common purpose of acting as intermediaries to facilitate requests between clients and target servers.

Proxy servers are defined by the Internet Engineering Task Force (IETF) at

Proxy server connections are specified by the W3C at

People who work for large organizations are probably familiar with the process of configuring their web browser, or other desktop applications that require Internet access to connect through a proxy. The proxy provides them with access to the Internet, while the network firewall protects the devices inside their network from intrusions.

A proxy server may eliminate the need for CORS in your application. As we shall see soon, a proxy server can have the same headers that make CORS possible, so that it sends and receives requests across domains.

Reasons to use a proxy

There are several reasons why you should place a proxy between your local domain and the target domain, which are as follows:

Avoid mixing up protocols

If your local domain application is served over SSL with HTTPS and you request a resource that is not served via SSL, the user may get a warning in the browser about mixing secure and non-secure content. Since the request to a proxy can also be made over SSL, there is no mixed content and the user sees no warning.

Some API platforms require proxies or CORS

An API hosted on a domain different from the local domain, a cloud-hosted API, or an **Enterprise Service Bus (ESB)** may require that cross-domain requests pass through a proxy or be handled by CORS. Apigee Edge, Mulesoft, and Google App Engine are platforms that require a proxy, or CORS, to pass requests. We will review solutions for specific platforms and applications in later chapters.

Getting through a local network firewall

In the same way that you may have to set up a browser to use a proxy to connect to the Internet through a local network firewall, any application that is behind the firewall of a local network will also need to connect to the proxy to request a resource with CORS that is outside the network.

Types of proxy server

You will need to create your own proxy server or use one that exists. We are not going to cover in detail how to set up every type of proxy server because to cover all the possible ways could be a book in itself!

A web search for cors proxy returns many results. Some of them describe APIs and services that require a CORS connection through a proxy. Other results provide solutions, libraries, and recipes for enabling a CORS request via proxy.

Beware that a lot of solutions listed as alternatives to CORS proxy use JSON-P, not CORS.

Creating a proxy server with Google App Engine

Google App Engine is an easy way to set up a proxy server for testing code and learning how to use a proxy.

If you use a public proxy server such as Google App Engine, then your data will not be private. A public proxy is suitable for testing, but you will need to use a secure proxy server that you own for production applications.

Create a New Application with Google App Engine:

There are detailed instructions at , including how to add authentication, because the proxy server will be publicly accessible. Even with added authentication, this proxy server is not sufficiently secure for a production application!

Reverse proxy server

A simple proxy server is known as a forward proxy, which retrieves a resource from another server and sends it to the original client making the request.

A reverse proxy server also retrieves resources on behalf of a client and returns them to the client as if they come from the proxy server itself, not from their actual origin.

You can create a proxy server on the same local server that hosts your application, or on another server you control.

Reverse proxy server with Apache VirtualHost and .htaccess

How you set up the reverse proxy server depends on your application environment, server software, and the type of application you are creating. Since many web applications are served through Apache, we will look at how to set up a reverse proxy sever using Apache.

An Apache proxy is created by using an Apache `VirtualHost` file and an `.htaccess` file.

 Refer to the Apache documentation for details about how to create a forward proxy or a reverse proxy ().

You also need to load the `modrewrite` and `modheaders` modules in Apache `httpd. conf`.

In httpd.conf:

* `LoadModule proxy_module /usr/lib/apache2/modules/mod_proxy.so`
* `LoadModule proxy_http_module /usr/lib/apache2/modules/mod_ proxy_http.so`
* `LoadModule headers_module /usr/lib/apache2/modules/mod_headers. so`

VirtualHost example code:

```
<virtualhost hostname:port>
ProxyRequests Off
ProxyPass / http://URL
ProxyPassReverse / http://URL
Header set Access-Control-Allow-Origin "*
Header set Access-Control-Allow-Headers "Origin, X-Requested-With,
Content-Type, Accept"
</virtualhost>
```

.htaccess example code:

```
RewriteEngine  on
RewriteBase /
RewriteRule  ^(.*)  http://URL  [P,L,QSA]
Header set Access-Control-Allow-Origin "*"
Header set Access-Control-Allow-Headers "Origin, Content-Type, Accept"
```

Note that in `VirtualHost` and `.htaccess` we set the headers needed for CORS:

```
Header set Access-Control-Allow-Origin "*
Header set Access-Control-Allow-Headers "Origin, X-Requested-With,
Content-Type, Accept"
```

Reverse proxy server in node.js

Single-page apps with Node.js are extremely popular. We will go into more detail about using CORS in node.js in *Chapter 7, CORS in Node.js*.

CORS anywhere () creates a reverse proxy with CORS headers added to the proxied request. It is a node package, that can be installed via **Node Package Manager (NPM)**.

 The `cors-anywhere` package can also be used on Heroku, a cloud-hosted application platform. More information about Heroku can be found at .

Heroku provides the proxy server. CORS anywhere can also be configured to use your own proxy server if you do not use Heroku.

Summary

Short and sweet, isn't it? We learned about proxy servers handling requests from our applications and forwarding the resource back to our application. We also saw scenarios such as avoiding mixing protocols, getting through local network firewalls, and API platforms that require proxies.

We also learned about forward proxy and reverse proxy. We walkedthrough the code that creates a reverse proxy server in Apache. Then we learned about using CORS anywhere to create a reverse proxy in node.js.

In the next chapter, we will learn about usability and security. We will learn ways to make sure that CORS can be used, including preflight. We saw that CORS itself does not provide much security, so we will look at how to secure your CORS application.

3
Usability and Security

In this chapter, you will learn how to implement CORS in various scenarios to enable access across domain boundaries.

We will discuss the following:

- CORS and XDomainRequest (IE 8 and 9) browser support
- Detecting AJAX support in the browser
- Using preflight to ensure usability and improve security
- The Access-Control-Allow-Origin header, with and without the wildcard
- HTTP request and response headers for usability and security
- CORS requests with credentials, and setting and reading cookies
- The CORS security cheat sheet by OWASP

 We use the term client to denote any user agent capable of making a CORS request. Typically, the client is the browser displaying the page making the request.

CORS usability

CORS is supported by all modern browsers, and XDomainRequest is its equivalent in Internet Explorer 8 and 9. Your code may include a switch to provide both the methods.

Using CORS requires planning: what resource(s) do you need to access, and how will you use them in your application?

Executing CORS requires preparation:

1. You must place the CORS header Access-Control-Allow-Origin on the page(s) on your target domain(s) for CORS to succeed.

2. A best practice is making sure that AJAX is supported by the client; otherwise, CORS with JavaScript will not be possible, and the function making the request can fail silently. Provide a handler in case AJAX is not supported.

3. Preflight is required for non-simple CORS requests. Preflight can detect potential problems that can make the actual request fail and can provide better security.

Browser support for CORS

All modern browsers support CORS. You can check for support at .

Global CORS support: 88.84%

Global XDomainRequest (IE 8,9): 4.72%

Total global CORS/XDomainRequest support: 93.56% as of March 2015

Browser	Supported minimum version number	Notes
Internet Explorer	10	XDomainRequest supported in IE 8 and 9
Firefox	34	
Chrome	31	
Safari	7.1	
Opera	26	
Opera Mini	No support	No CORS support in Opera Mini 5.0 – 8.0
IOS Safari	7.1	
Chrome for Android	40	
Android Browser	4.1	

The following are the known issues:

IE10 and above does not send cookies when `withCredential=true` (IE Bug #759587)

IE10 and above does not make a CORS request if port is the only difference (IE Bug #781303)

Android and some old versions of WebKit do not support Access-Control-Expose-Headers ()

Detecting AJAX support in the browser

The first thing we do in our CORS request is to make sure that AJAX is supported in the client browser. If the user has disabled JavaScript in the browser, then AJAX is also disabled. Disabling JavaScript is rare since so many applications depend on JavaScript.

We covered the code for creating the AJAX `XMLHttpRequest` (`XHR`) in *Chapter 1, Why You Need CORS*:

```
// Create the XHR object.
function createCORSRequest(method, url) {
  var xhr = new XMLHttpRequest();
  if ("withCredentials" in xhr) {
    // XHR for Chrome/Firefox/Opera/Safari and IE >= 10
    xhr.open(method, url, true);
  } else if (typeof XDomainRequest != "undefined") {
    // XDomainRequest for IE <= 9
    xhr = new XDomainRequest();
    xhr.open(method, url);
  } else {
    // CORS not supported
    xhr = null;
  }
  return xhr;
}
```

If the response includes `withCredentials`, or `typeof XDomainRequest!="undefined"` for Internet Explorer 8 and 9, we return the XHR response. Otherwise, we cannot use AJAX; therefore, we cannot use CORS.

Consider adding some kind of error-handling method in case JavaScript is not supported. You may, for example, store the XHR response from a previous session, or you can have some code that does something else, such as displaying a message telling the user that JavaScript may be disabled, with instructions for re-enabling it. The <noscript> tag can be used to provide code when JavaScript is not supported. The request function should also have an error handler to do something if CORS is not supported.

If you do nothing to handle this exception, your application may appear to be broken when the problem is caused by the client configuration and is beyond your control.

Using preflight for non-simple CORS requests

Preflight is a request the XHR object makes to ensure it's actually able to make another request.

In *Chapter 1, Why You Need CORS*, we learned that

The CORS specification requires browsers to preflight requests that do the following:

- Use request methods other than GET, POST, or HEAD
- Have custom headers
- Have Content-Type other than text/plain, application/x-www-form-urlencoded, or multipart/form-data

Let's look at a JavaScript preflight request example. It PUTs a custom header with the value customValue on the page defined in the targetdomain URL at somePath. Since it uses the PUT method AND sets a custom header, preflight is required. We do not have to test for AJAX support in the actual request because without AJAX support, the preflight request would fail:

```
var url = 'http://targetdomain/somePath';
var xhr = createCORSRequest('PUT', url);
xhr.setRequestHeader('X-Custom-Header', 'customValue');
xhr.send();
```

The client sends the following information to the target domain:

```
OPTIONS /cors HTTP/1.1
Origin: http://localdomain
Access-Control-Request-Method: PUT
Access-Control-Request-Headers: X-Custom-Header
Host: targetdomain
Accept-Language: en-US
Connection: keep-alive
```

```
User-Agent: [info about the client making the request]
```

The target domain server sends back the response:

```
Access-Control-Allow-Origin: http://localdomain (this header is set
explicitly)
Access-Control-Allow-Methods: GET, POST, PUT
Access-Control-Allow-Headers: X-Custom-Header
Content-Type: text/html; charset=utf-8
```

This is a successful response to the preflight request. The PUT method is allowed and so is the X-Custom-Header method. Then the browser makes the actual request:

```
PUT /cors HTTP/1.1
Origin: http://localdomain
Host: targetdomain
X-Custom-Header: customValue
Accept-Language: en-US
Connection: keep-alive
User-Agent: [info about the client making the request]
```

The targetdomain server responds:

```
Access-Control-Allow-Origin: http://localdomain.com
Content-Type: text/html; charset=utf-8
```

 No responseText is returned because the request PUTs a custom header; it does not request anything in return via GET.

If the server at the targetdomain server denies the CORS request, it returns a generic response (generally HTTP 200), without any CORS headers (Access-Control-Allow-Origin). The server may deny the request if the HTTP method or headers requested in the preflight are not valid. With no CORS-specific headers in the preflight response, the client doesn't make the actual request.

 When writing a preflight request, test for the specific method(s) and header(s) that you need to use in the actual request. Also, check the content type in the preflight response if you need to use any Content-Type other than text/plain, application/x-www-form-urlencoded, or multipart/form-data. A preflight will always fail if the target domain does not return the CORS header, Access-Control-Allow-Origin, with the local domain.

If you failed to first make a preflight request, a non-simple request would fail automatically.

The HTTP request headers

Clients send HTTP request headers when making a request. In a simple request, you do not have to specify any headers; the CORS request sends the required headers automatically. When making a preflight request, you may define a header to be used.

These are the HTTP request headers:

```
Origin: <origin>
```

In the example preflight request, the client sends the origin, `http://localdomain`, automatically.

> The origin can be the empty string; this is useful, for example, if the request is from a data URL.

```
Access-Control-Request-Method: <method>
```

A preflight request tells the `targetdomain` server which HTTP method will be used when the actual request is made. In the preflight example, the client sends `Access-Control-Request-Method: PUT` because we specified `var xhr=createCORSRequest('PUT', url)` in the request.

```
Access-Control-Request-Headers: <header-name1>, <header-name2> ...
```

A preflight request tells the `targetdomain` server which HTTP headers will be used when the actual request is made. In the preflight example, the client sends `Access-Control-Request-Headers: X-Custom-Header` because we specified `xhr.setRequestHeader('X-Custom-Header', 'customValue')` in the request.

HTTP response headers

Servers send back HTTP response headers for access control requests as defined by the CORS specification. These headers may be used in preflight and also to enhance security. We will learn about enhancing security in CORS in the next section.

These are the HTTP response headers:

```
Access-Control-Allow-Origin: <localdomain> | *
```

This header tells the application on the local domain that it is an allowed origin to make a request. Values are either a list of all allowed domains or the wildcard *, which allows any domain. In practice, most clients do not recognize a list of domains, so only one domain or the wildcard may be used. Avoid using the wildcard if possible because it creates security risks.

This header sends a list of headers that the client is allowed to access:

```
Access-Control-Expose-Headers: X-Custom-Header, X-Another-Custom-Header
```

This header sends the number of seconds a preflight request can be cached:

```
Access-Control-Max-Age: <seconds>
```

The following header indicates whether or not the response to the request can be exposed when the credentials flag is true. In a preflight request, this indicates whether or not the actual request can be made using `withCredentials`:

```
Access-Control-Allow-Credentials: true | false
```

 Simple requests are not preflighted; so, if a simple request is made for a resource `withCredentials` and the `Access-Control-Allow-Credentials` header is not returned, the response is ignored by the browser.

The following header is returned in response to a preflight request. In the preflight example, the `targetdomain` server returns `Access-Control-Allow-Methods: GET, POST, PUT`:

```
Access-Control-Allow-Methods: <method1>, <method2> …
```

The following header returns the name(s) of the HTTP headers that can be used when making the actual request. In the preflight example, the `targetdomain` server returns `Access-Control-Allow-Headers: X-Custom-Header`:

```
Access-Control-Allow-Headers: <header-name1>, <header-name2> …
```

Enhancing security in CORS

CORS by itself does not provide any security, except for the domain allowed in the `Access-Control-Allow-Origin` header.

Some recommended practices for better security when using CORS are as follows:

- Place the CORS header only on page(s) that need it; do not add the header across site
- Use `Access-Control-Allow-Origin: *` only for publicly accessible static resources that do not include sensitive information or modify data

Limiting access when using the Access-Control-Allow-Origin, * wildcard

Although the CORS specification suggests that a list of allowed domains may be provided, in practice, very few clients support a list of allowed domains. Therefore, if you need to allow more than one domain, you must allow all domains with the `Access-Control-Allow-Origin, * wildcard`. Then, any domain, even the ones that are not intended, can make a CORS request to the page with the header.

You must provide additional security when using the wildcard if you want to prevent CORS requests from unintended domains.

> Check release notes for browsers to find out when each browser implements support for a list of allowed domains. Eventually, the list suggested in the CORS specification will be widely implemented, making the wildcard unnecessary.

Trusting the HTTP_ORIGIN header is not recommended

One way to check the origin of the server making the request is to inspect the `HTTP_ORIGIN` header and compare it with the `Access-Control-Allow-Origin` header.

The `HTTP_ORIGIN` header only indicates that the request is from a particular domain; it does not guarantee it. For example, a script can spoof the `HTTP_ORIGIN` header.

You may be tempted to to trust the HTTP_ORIGIN header, but it can be spoofed on an untrusted domain, so it is not secure:

```php
<?php
    if($_SERVER['HTTP_ORIGIN'] == "http://localdomain")
    {
      header('Access-Control-Allow-Origin: http://localdomain');
      // Origin of localdomain matches allowed value
      do something using with CORS
    }
    else
    {
     // Origin does not match
     do something without CORS
    }
?>
```

You may use code like this, perhaps, if the target domain resource does not contain any confidential information. It cannot be trusted for security.

> Best practices for CORS security recommend never using the wildcard in the Access-Control-Allow-Origin header. Consider this when designing your applications.

Requests with credentials

Requests with credentials use HTTP Cookies and HTTP authentication information. A specific flag has to be set on the XMLHttpRequest header object when it is invoked to make a withCredentials request.

When responding to a credentialed request, the targetdomain server must specify a domain. The following example would fail if the header used the wild card Access-Control-Allow-Origin, *. Since the Access-Control-Allow-Origin header value in the response is http://localdomain, the responseText request is returned to the client making the request.

The following code makes a request with credentials. It creates the request XHR object. When the requestWithCredentials() function is invoked, a request is made using the GET method, withCredentials. If the response returns the header Access-Control-Allow-Credentials: true, then the responseText request is passed to the handlerFunction() function. If the Access-Control-Allow-Credentials header is set to false, or is missing, the request fails.

```
var xhr = new XMLHttpRequest();
var url = 'http://targetdomain/path-to-credentialed-content/';
function requestWithCredentials(){
  if(xhr) {
    xhr.open('GET', url, true);
    xhr.withCredentials = true;
    xhr.onreadystatechange = handlerFunction;
    xhr.send();
  }
}
```

Request from client:

```
GET path-to-credentialed-content/ HTTP/1.1
Host: targetdomain
User-Agent: [info about the client making the request]
Accept: text/html,application/xhtml+xml,application/
xml;q=0.9,*/*;q=0.8
Accept-Language: en-us,en;q=0.5
Accept-Encoding: gzip,deflate
Accept-Charset: ISO-8859-1,utf-8;q=0.7,*;q=0.7
Connection: keep-alive
Referer: http://localdomain/page-making-request
Origin: http://localdomain
Cookie: [cookie information to be set on Target Domain]
```

Response from Target Domain server:

```
HTTP/1.1 200 OK
Date: Mon, 01 Dec 2008 01:34:52 GMT
Server: [server info]
X-Powered-By: PHP/5.2.6
Access-Control-Allow-Origin: http://localdomain
Access-Control-Allow-Credentials: true
Cache-Control: no-cache
Pragma: no-cache
Set-Cookie: [cookie info on Target Domain page]
Vary: Accept-Encoding, Origin
Content-Encoding: gzip
Content-Length: 106
Keep-Alive: timeout=2, max=100
Connection: Keep-Alive
Content-Type: text/plain
[responseText: text returned via GET method]
```

As given in , you can try a request `withCredentials` at . You can inspect the page source and the script in the `<head>` tag of the page, including the request and the handler function.

This page requests a resource on the target domain that sets a counter cookie there. The resource is requested using `withCredentials` in the `XMLHttpRequest` header. The `responseText` request returned by the target domain varies depending on the value of the cookie set on the target domain page.

The `responseText` is processed in the `handler()` function and looks like this after clicking the button to make the request three times:

Hello—I know you or something a lot like you! You have been to aruner.net at least 2 time(s) before!

Also note that the target domain page specified in the request is generated by a server-side script that is not detectable in the page source; that page contains only the content returned in the `responseText`. You can reload this URL and see the text change each time the page is requested.

CORS security cheat sheet by OWASP

The **Open Web Application Security Project (OWASP)** makes the following recommendations for security in CORS applications. Source URL:

Summary

In this chapter, we learned the following:

- Total global `CORS`/`XDomainRequest` support is 93.56% as of March 2015
- AJAX support in the browser must be checked, and a handler should be used in case it is not supported
- A preflight request before the actual request can ensure usability and improve security

- Avoid using the wildcard in the he `Access-Control-Allow-Origin` header
- HTTP requests and response headers play a role in usability and security
- CORS requests `withcredentials` provide better security
- When making CORS requests `withCredentials`, we can set and reading cookies on the target domain
- The CORS security cheat sheet by OWASP provides a checklist of best practices

In the next chapter, you will learn about using CORS in popular Content Management Systems, such as WordPress, Drupal, Joomla, and Adobe CQ.

4

CORS in Popular Content Management Frameworks

In this chapter, we will learn about the following:

- Enabling CORS in WordPress, Drupal, Joomla!, and **Adobe Experience Manager (AEM)**
- Enabling CORS in the WordPress.com SAAS platform
- WordPress plugins for CORS and methods using the API
- Drupal modules for CORS and methods using the API
- The AEM package `com.adobe.cq.social.commons.cors`
- Using rulesets in AEM to add CORS headers
- Configuring the Sling Referrer filter in the AEM CRX Console

 In 2013, Adobe Systems renamed the Adobe CQ WCM to Adobe Experience Manager (also known as Adobe AEM or just AEM).

Incoming CORS requests

Web content management frameworks are often integrated with external platforms, APIs, and services. When the external source is hosted on a different domain, CORS is used to allow requests from the external local domain to the target domain of the web content management framework, without needing a proxy. We will look at techniques for allowing these requests.

When making a CORS request from the web content management framework as the local domain to a different target domain, it is either handled with custom code using the methods we covered in the earlier chapters, or a plugin may implement the headers and methods needed for the requests.

SAAS or self-hosted?

All the major content management frameworks offer a **Software As A Service (SAAS)** hosted/managed option. Since you do not actually control the server, and scripting is limited, implementing CORS may be difficult, or sometimes impossible.

In the SAAS platform WordPress.com, we shall see that CORS is very limited, and authenticated requests require explicit permission by the current user.

The Drupal SAAS platforms Drupal Gardens and Acquia Cloud Site Factory do not provide a way to implement CORS. There have been feature requests for adding CORS capability, so it may become possible.

It's unclear whether CORS is possible in the SAAS versions of Joomla! and Adobe Experience Manager.

The demand for the capability of CORS will likely be satisfied in these SAAS platforms eventually, so we recommend contacting support and asking them explicitly whether CORS can be implemented.

CORS in WordPress

WordPress can be self hosted, or you could use WordPress.com, which is the hosted/managed SaaS platform for creating WordPress sites. Although incoming and outgoing CORS requests are possible in the self-hosted WordPress, the WordPress.com platform only allows incoming requests.

Limited support for CORS in SAAS WordPress.com

WordPress.com provides a REST API, which can allow incoming CORS requests via JavaScript/jQuery only; other languages are not supported.

You need to whitelist the domains you want to allow to make requests to your application in the dashboard for the site. Authenticated and unauthenticated requests are supported.

 The REST API provides a way for other domains to interact with the WordPress.com application. Requests are made to the URI , which is the API endpoint for WordPress.com. There is no provision for making a CORS request from WordPress.com to another domain. That is a limitation of using the WordPress.com SAAS compared with the self-hosted WordPress.

Unauthenticated GET requests to WordPress.com

You can make unauthenticated GET requests with a simple HTTP request:

```
jQuery.get(http://public-api.wordpress.com/rest/v1/sites/
  www.samplesite.com/", function( response ) {
    // response contains the HTML from the requested page
} );
```

Authenticated requests to WordPress.com

In an authenticated request on WordPress.com, the current user must explicitly authorize the application in order to generate an OAuth token, which then allows the CORS request.

 Because the current user must explicitly allow an authenticated CORS request on WordPress.com, the request cannot be made in the background without prior consent by the current user.

To make authenticated requests, follow the implicit section of the OAuth documentation on WordPress.com to get a user token:

The authorization endpoint is .

The token request endpoints is .

Whitelist origins in the application manager

To make authenticated requests, you need to whitelist the domain(s) that will make the requests. You can do this while creating or configuring your application with the application manager in your site's dashboard.

In the following example, is whitelisted as the local domain, making the request to the WordPress.com site the target domain. List one URL per line.

Get/Store user access token

To act on a user's behalf and make calls from your API, you need an access token. If you don't already have an access token for the user visiting your website, you need to obtain a token as explained in the implicit section of the WordPress.com OAuth documentation. WordPress.com implements Oauth2.

To get an access token, you need to go through the access token flow and prompt the user to authorize your application to act on their behalf. You need to send the user to the authorization endpoint. Here's an example request: .

Access tokens can be requested per blog, per user, or as a global token per user. In addition to the global tokens, there are certain endpoints (for example, likes and follows) where you can use a user's token on any blog to act on their behalf.

Tokens expire after two weeks, and users need to authenticate with your application again once the token expires.

As the owner of the application, you can authenticate with the password `grant_type`, which allows you to skip the authorization step by logging in with your WordPress.com username and password. This is only available to you as the owner of the application, and not to any other user. It is meant for testing purposes only.

Validating the token for security

Validating the token before making the actual request is recommended to ensure that it belongs to your application and the user you are authenticating. From the domain making the requests, use the endpoint , and pass your client ID and the token.

Example validation:

If the token provided is not authorized for your application, the endpoint will return an error. If the token is valid, the response is a JSON-encoded string with the user ID and scope of the token:

```
{
    "client_id": "your client ID",
    "user_id": "user ID",
    "blog_id": "blog ID",
    "scope": "scope of the token"
}
```

Making the request

When making the request, pass the access token as a header with the name "Authorization" and the value "BEARER " + access_token.

Here is an example of a POST request, which creates a new post on the WordPress. com site, using the token as a header:

```
jQuery.ajax( {
    url: 'https://public-api.wordpress.com/rest/v1/sites/' + site_id +
'/posts/new',
    type: 'POST',
    data: { content: 'your_content' },
    beforeSend : function( xhr ) {
        xhr.setRequestHeader( 'Authorization', 'BEARER ' + access_
token );
    },
    success: function( response ) {
        // response
    }
} );
```

CORS in self-hosted WordPress

CORS can be used in self-hosted WordPress applications using standard CORS techniques for headers and requests, or by adding helper plugins for CORS.

Adding the Access-Control-Allow-Origin header in a template

You can add the CORS header to all the pages in the WordPress application by editing the `header.php` file in your theme. The following example adds the header whitelisting requests from all domains:

```php
<?php /** @package WordPress @subpackage Default_Theme **/
header("Access-Control-Allow-Origin: *");
?>
```

> Be conscious of security and best practices when adding the CORS header globally in the template. You can add a specified domain instead of the wildcard "*" or some other code that authenticates the domain making the request before allowing access. You may also add logic to only send the header on specific paths. Example code to authenticate the domain making a request has been provided in the previous chapters.

WordPress plugins for CORS

There are two plugins available to implement CORS in WordPress. Install them the usual way by uploading them to the `wp-content/plugins` directory and activating them in the plugins menu.

> The first plugin, WP-CORS, appears to be more actively supported, and therefore, it is the recommended one, unless you need to use CORS with the WordPress XML-RPC API.

WP-CORS plugin for WordPress

This plugin provides an admin page to add the domains allowed to make CORS requests to the WordPress site and add the `Access-Control-Allow-Origin` header.

Information about the WP-CORS plugin:

Version 0.2 Requires WordPress 3.6 or higher; Compatible up to: 4.0.1

Last Updated: 2014-10-5

Active Installs: 100+

The WP-CORS plugin URL is .

The following screenshot is the plugin's administrative screen, showing the input field for allowed domains:

 When adding multiple domains, be conscious of the limited support by client browsers for the Access-Control-Allow-Origin header with multiple domains.

Allow CORS XML-RPC plugin for WordPress

This plugin provides support for CORS with the WordPress XML-RPC API.

XML-RPC is a protocol created in 1998 using XML in an HTTP-POST request. It evolved into **Simple Object Access Protocol (SOAP)**.

In WordPress, XML-RPC is used to post to the WordPress site from external blogging applications.

Here is the XML-RPC specification: and information about using XML-RPC in WordPress: .

Unless you need to use CORS with XML-RPC in WordPress, the WP-CORS plugin or custom code should be used to add allowed domains in CORS headers.

Information about the Allow CORS XMP-RPC plugin:
Version 0.1 Requires WordPress 3.6.0 or higher; Compatible up to: 3.6.1
Last Updated: 2013-10-18
Active Installs: 80+

Allow CORS XML-RPC plugin URL: .

No screenshot for the Allow CORS XMP-RPC plugin is provided on WordPress.org.

CORS in Drupal

Custom code is the best way to implement CORS in Drupal, using techniques we have covered. There are also some contributed Drupal modules for CORS. Be mindful of Drupal core API differences among versions: Drupal 6, 7, 8. When Drupal 8 is released, support for Drupal 6 will end.

Enabling CORS in Drupal with custom code

CORS headers may be added to endpoints created in a custom module or in the `template.php` file in your theme.

The CORS headers can be added:

- With the Drupal API function `drupal_add_http_header`
- By configuring `.htaccess` to send headers, for example, using Apache's `mod.headers`
- By explicitly setting the header with code in a custom module or theme template

Using the drupal_add_http_header function

The following custom function adds CORS headers in Drupal 7 for a JSON application, with the wildcard to allow requests from all domains, and allows GET, PUT, POST, and DELETE methods:

```
function set_custom_headers()
 {
  drupal_add_http_header('Content-Type', 'application/json');
  drupal_add_http_header('Access-Control-Allow-Origin', "*");
  drupal_add_http_header('Access-Control-Allow-Methods',
'GET,PUT,POST,DELETE');
 }
```

Drupal_add_http_header is a core Drupal 7 API function. It is deprecated in Drupal 8; instead, use \Symfony\Component\ HttpFoundation\Response->headers->set(). Use drupal_set_ header in Drupal 6.

Adding CORS support with .htaccess

The following code in .htaccess enables the POST, GET, and OPTIONS methods and allows request from all origins with the wildcard:

```
<IfModule mod_headers.c>
  Header always set Access-Control-Allow-Origin "*"
  Header always set Access-Control-Allow-Methods "GET, POST, OPTIONS"
  Header always set Access-Control-Allow-Headers "accept, content-
type"
  Header always set Access-Control-Allow-Credentials "true"
</IfModule>
```

You may also want to intercept the OPTIONS calls in .htaccess:

```
RewriteEngine On
RewriteCond %{REQUEST_METHOD} OPTIONS
RewriteRule ^(.*)$ $1 [R=200,L,E=HTTP_ORIGIN:%{HTTP:ORIGIN}]]
```

These changes in .htaccess have been proposed for Drupal core. Security concerns have been raised about using the wild card for Access-Control-Allow-Origin in the .htaccess file that is distributed in Drupal core.

Adding the CORS headers with custom code

You can also add the header explicitly in a file that serves as the endpoint in the Drupal application, using standard CORS methods. For example, if your endpoint is a PHP file, add the Access-Control-Allow-Origin header as follows:

```
<?php
header('Access-Control-Allow-Origin: http://localdomain.com');
?>";
```

Drupal contributed modules for CORS

It's impossible to document all Drupal contributed modules that support CORS. The Drupal community is very active, and new modules are added constantly. We will look at a few key modules.

Drupal CORS module

The CORS module works with Drupal 7 and a Drupal 8 version is planned.

The CORS module project page URL is .

The CORS module provides an administration screen to define headers that will be sent for specific paths in the Drupal application. It's also possible to define headers globally for all paths.

This module is mainly useful if you only need to add headers, for example, when you are integrating with an API or service that requires adding CORS headers in your Drupal application. For most purposes, you will probably be adding a custom module for your integration, and it is preferable to add the CORS headers there the standard way.

The documentation for the module explains the usage:

A list of paths and corresponding domains to enable for CORS. Multiple entries should be separated by a comma. Enter one value per line separated by a pipe, in this order:

Internal path:

- Access-Control-Allow-Origin. Use <mirror> to echo back the Origin header.
- Access-Control-Allow-Methods
- Access-Control-Allow-Headers
- Access-Control-Allow-Credentials

Examples:

- `*|http://example.com`
- `api|http://example.com:8080 http://example.com`
- `api/*|<mirror>,https://example.com`
- `api/*|<mirror>|POST|Content-Type,Authorization|true`

The `<mirror>` token will only insert a value if the request is made with the Origin header set. It is similar to using the wildcard since any request made with an Origin header will be allowed. For security, additional logic in code should be used to determine whether the value of the Origin header is included in a list of allowed origins.

A line-by-line explanation of the following screenshot of the administration page for the module is as follows:

In the first line, a global setting is made with * to send the `Access-Control-Allow-Origin` header for two domains: `http://example.com` and `https://example.com` on all paths in the Drupal application.

> Note that a space-separated list of allowed origins is part of the CORS specification, but it may not be supported by all client browsers. Our recommendation is to give one allowed domain, or handle multiple allowed domains with logic in code that is external to the `Access-Control-Allow-Origin` header.

In the second line, the headers are sent only for the `admin/config/services/*` path, and the allowed domain is `http://somedomain.com`.

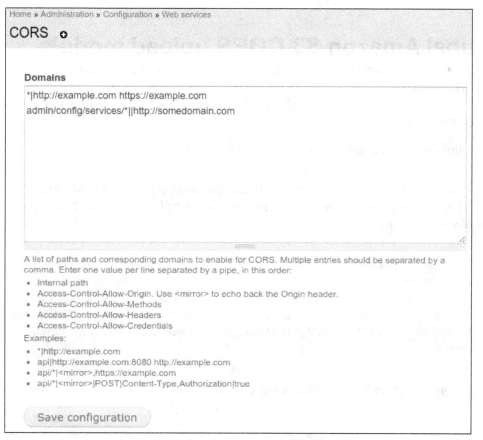

Domain and path to enable CORS

Be careful to avoid adding multiple headers for the same path. If you define headers globally with the wildcard * (as you can see in the first line in the screenshot), then you cannot define any header for specific paths. You will get a PHP warning in Drupal 7:

Warning: Header may not contain more than a single header, new line detected in `drupal_send_headers()`.

Drupal CDN module

The CDN module is a generic integrator for serving files via **Content Delivery Network (CDN)** in Drupal 6 and 7. In version >=2.3 it supports CORS. It's unclear whether this module will be ported to Drupal 8. When using Amazon S3, the Amazon S3 CORS Upload module is recommended instead.

Drupal CDN module project page URL: .

Drupal Amazon S3 CORS upload module

The Drupal Amazon S3 CORS upload module is only used to implement CORS with S3 in Drupal 7. The AmazonS3 module (upon which this module is dependent) replaces the Drupal filesystem with the S3 bucket. It's unclear whether this module will be ported to Drupal 8.

The following description is provided at the project page: :

> *This module works in conjunction with the amazons3 module to provide direct to S3 uploading from your browser. Bypassing the Drupal file system and storing all files in S3 only.*

> *When using this method to upload files to S3 files are uploaded directly from the user's browser to S3 and not stored in the local file system. This can be nice in that you don't have to upload files to Drupal first and then have Drupal transfer them to S3 for you. The module then stores a managed file record in Drupal for the new file and the file is then treated just like any file that was uploaded via the normal means.*

> *The module provides a new field widget for file fields.*

CORS in Drupal 8 core

Drupal 8 supports CORS through `XMLHttpRequest` by including jQuery 2.1.0 (or greater) in `core/assets/jquery`:

```
support.cors = !!xhrSupported && ( "withCredentials" in xhrSupported
);
```

There has been discussion on supporting CORS using other methods in Drupal 8 core. CORS support, except through jQuery, is not included in the 8.0.x release, but it may be added as a feature in the later releases of Drupal 8.

CORS in Joomla!

To enable CORS in Joomla!, you need to add the standard CORS header(s). There are a few ways to add the header(s), which are covered in the following sections.

setHeader in JApplication web

Since Joomla! version 11.4, the core method to set headers is `setHeader` in the base class `JapplicationWeb`, which can be used to set the `Access-Control-Allow-Origin` header and can be used to set other headers.

The following example allows access from all domains with the wildcard:

```
setHeader('Access-Control-Allow-Origin', '*', true) : \JApplicationWeb
```

You may find discussions regarding the use of `JResponse::setHeader` for CORS in Joomla!; however, it has been deprecated since Joomla! Version 11.4. Use `setHeader` in the base class `JApplicationWeb` instead.

matware-libraries on GitHub

Although we could not find any Joomla! extensions available to configure allowed origins from the web admin, there is a project on GitHub named `matware-libraries`, which adds the `Access-Control-Allow-Origin` header. Matware-libraries also add OAuth2 and WebSocket support to Joomla!. The GitHub project for matware-libraries URL is .

Allowing CORS in the .htaccess file

It has been suggested that the CORS headers for XHR requests and for cross-domain images can be configured in the Joomla! `.htaccess` file.

The following code comes from a blog post at :

```
# -------------------------------------------------------------------
---
# Cross-domain AJAX requests
# -------------------------------------------------------------------
---

# Serve cross-domain Ajax requests, disabled by default.
# enable-cors.org
# code.google.com/p/html5security/wiki/CrossOriginRequestSecurity

#   <IfModule mod_headers.c>
#     Header set Access-Control-Allow-Origin "*"
#   </IfModule>


# -------------------------------------------------------------------
---
# CORS-enabled images (@crossorigin)
# -------------------------------------------------------------------
---

# Send CORS headers if browsers request them; enabled by default for
images.
# developer.mozilla.org/en/CORS_Enabled_Image
# blog.chromium.org/2011/07/using-cross-domain-images-in-webgl-and.
html
# hacks.mozilla.org/2011/11/using-cors-to-load-webgl-textures-from-
cross-domain-images/
# wiki.mozilla.org/Security/Reviews/crossoriginAttribute

<IfModule mod_setenvif.c>
  <IfModule mod_headers.c>
    # mod_headers, y u no match by Content-Type?!
    <FilesMatch "\.(gif|png|jpe?g|svg|svgz|ico|webp)$">
      SetEnvIf Origin ":" IS_CORS
      Header set Access-Control-Allow-Origin "*" env=IS_CORS
    </FilesMatch>
  </IfModule>
</IfModule>
```

Note that this example adds the headers to every page request with the wildcard. Although the wildcard could be replaced with specific domain(s), best practices for security in CORS do not recommend adding the header to pages where CORS is not needed. Although the author of this code recommends adding the configuration to the web server rather than in `.htaccess`, the same security concerns remain without limiting which paths have the header.

CORS in Adobe Experience Manager

While the previous sections examined using CORS in frameworks built with PHP, Adobe Experience Manager is built with Java.

In 2013, Adobe systems renamed the Adobe CQ WCM to Adobe Experience Manager (also known as Adobe AEM or just AEM).

AEM has a Java package for CORS. Another option is to allow domains to post to Sling in the CRX console; when domains are trusted this way, CORS is unnecessary. In some cases, such as when using Scene 7, CORS headers may need to be added with rulesets.

The com.adobe.cq.social.commons.cors package

AEM includes a package named `com.adobe.cq.social.commons.cors`. The package contains four classes:

Classes in com.adobe.cq.social.commons.cors	Description
CORSAuthenticationFilter	Adds CORS headers to HTTP responses
CORSAuthInfoPostProcessor	CORS authentication post processor
CORSConfig	Singleton configuration holder so that both the CORS filter and CORS post processor have access to the system settings
CORSConstants	CORS Constant strings, extends object

Methods in the CORSAuthenticationFilter class

Use this class to add CORS headers to HTTP responses. There are four methods:

- `init` extends the `init` method in `javax.servlet.Filter`
- `doFilter` extends `javax.servlet.ServletRequest, javax.servlet. ServletResponse, javax.servlet.FilterChain`
- `destroy` extends destroy in the `javax.servlet.Filter` interface
- `activate` activates the `ComponentContext`

Usage of methods in the CORSAuthenticationFilter class:

```
public void init(javax.servlet.FilterConfig filterConfig)
public void doFilter(javax.servlet.ServletRequest request,
                     javax.servlet.ServletResponse response,
                     javax.servlet.FilterChain chain)
public void destroy()
protected void activate(ComponentContext context)
```

Methods In the CORSConfig class

Use this class to get the CORSConfig instance, test if CORS is enabled, and enable/disable CORS. There are three methods:

- `getInstance` gets the `CORSConfig` instance
- `isEnable` retrieves a boolean value to test if CORS is enabled
- `setCORSEnabling` sets a boolean value true/false to enable/disable CORS

Usage of methods in the CORSConfig class:

```
public static CORSConfig getInstance()
public boolean isEnable()
public void setCORSEnabling(boolean value)
```

Methods in the CORSAuthInfoPostProcessor class

The `CORSAuthInfoPostProcessor` class has only one method, which extends the `HttpServletRequest` and `HttpServletResponse` methods in the `AuthenticationInfoPostProcessor` interface.

Usage of the post process method in the CORSAuthInfoPostProcessor class:

```
public void postProcess(AuthenticationInfo info,
                        javax.servlet.http.HttpServletRequest request,
                        javax.servlet.http.HttpServletResponse
response)
```

Adding CORS headers in Scene 7 with a ruleset

Scene 7 is a dynamic media platform for AEM.

It has been suggested that the `Access-Control-Allow-Origin` headers need to be added in Scene 7 by defining a ruleset with expressions that match your allowed domains.

The following ruleset has an expression for each of the subdomains for typical deployment environments (staging, production, development):

```xml
<?xml version="1.0" encoding="UTF-8"?>
<ruleset>
    <rule OnMatch="continue">
      <expression>.a=pft</expression>
      <header Name="Access-Control-Allow-Origin" Action="set">pft.
company.com</header>
    </rule>
    <rule>
      <expression>.a=www</expression>
      <header Name="Access-Control-Allow-Origin" Action="set">www.
company.com</header>
    </rule>
    <rule>
      <expression>.a=dev</expression>
      <header Name="Access-Control-Allow-Origin" Action="set">dev.
company.com</header>
    </rule>
</ruleset>
```

It's not possible to use the wildcard, so each allowed domain requires a separate rule.

A similar technique could add the allowed domains by storing them in a variable:

```xml
<?xml version="1.0" encoding="UTF-8"?>
<!DOCTYPE ruleset SYSTEM "RuleSet.dtd">
<ruleset>
<rule OnMatch="continue">
        <expression>\$CORS=</expression>
        <header Name="Access-Control-Allow-Origin">$CORS$</header>
</rule>
</ruleset>
```

Configuring the Sling Referrer Filter in the CRX Console

The CRX console administers Experience Services--Core (CRX) with its embedded Content Repository. Apache Sling is an open source web framework for the Java platform designed to create content-centric applications.

You can configure domains in the Sling Referrer filter of the CRX Console that are allowed to post to Sling Post. For security, do not allow any external domains that you don't have control over.

[When domains are trusted in in the Sling Referrer filter, using CORS is not necessary.]

Summary

We have learned a lot about applying CORS in various content management systems. Let's do a recap.

You learned how to allow incoming CORS requests in WordPress, Drupal, Joomla!, and Adobe Expression Manager. You also learned that outgoing CORS requests in these frameworks should use custom code or existing plugins, apart from the fact that WordPress.com SAAS has limited CORS capability. We discussed how CORS support in other SAAS versions of these frameworks is uncertain, but it may become implemented due to demand.

We looked at two plugins for CORS in WordPress: one for adding headers, and the other enables CORS in the WordPress XML-RPC API. We also looked at adding CORS headers with custom code in the WordPress theme template.

We looked at a few Drupal modules for CORS. The CORS module adds headers mapped to paths. The CDN module supports CORS when using a Content Delivery Network. The Amazon S3 upload module implements CORS when using Amazon S3. We also looked at setting headers in custom code or in Drupal theme templates.

We looked at a few ways to implement CORS in Joomla!. setHeader in JApplication Web adds headers. The matware-libraries project also adds headers. It has been suggested that headers may be added in Joomla! by modifying the .htaccess file or server configuration.

We looked at a few ways to implement CORS in Adobe Experience Manager. We looked at methods in the `com.adobe.cq.social.commons.cors package`. We looked at adding headers with rulesets, which may be necessary when using Adobe Scene 7. We looked at whitelisting requests from domains by configuring the Sling Referrer filter in the CRX Console, making CORS unnecessary.

In the next chapter, you will learn about using CORS in Windows frameworks and environments.

5
CORS in Windows

In this chapter, we are going to discuss how to implement CORS on the Windows platform. The Windows platform includes IIS and ASP.NET Web API applications, as well as the Windows Communication Foundation.

We will learn about:

- How to set the `Access-Control-Allow-Origin` header globally in `web.config` for Windows IIS Server
- How to install and use the `Microsoft ASP.NET Web API Cross-Origin Support` package, including:
    - Setting CORS policies with the `EnableCorsAttribute` class
    - Disabling CORS policies with the `DisableCors` attribute
    - Creating dynamic CORS policies with the `Custom CORS Policy Attribute` class
    - Creating dynamic CORS policies driven by logic with the custom CORS policy provider factory
- How to use CORS in **Windows Communication Foundation (WCF)**
- Note that Edge and Internet Explorer 10 fully support `XmlHttpRequest` `withCredentials`, IE 8 and 9 use `XDomainRequest` instead of `XmlHttpRequest`, and IE 7 and lesser versions do not support CORS at all

Incoming CORS requests

Web applications are often integrated with external platforms, APIs, and services. When the external source is hosted on a different domain, CORS is used to allow requests from the external local domain to the target domain, without an intermediate proxy. We will look at techniques for allowing cross-domain requests in Windows applications and servers. When making a CORS request from the Windows application as the local domain to a different target domain, it is handled with custom code using the methods we have covered in earlier chapters.

How to set the Access-Control-Allow-Origin header globally in Windows IIS Server

Although it is possible to set the Access-Control-Allow-Origin header value globally in web.config for Windows IIS Server, the Microsoft ASP.NET Web API Cross-Origin Support package provides classes and interfaces for the sophisticated handling of CORS requests.

In general, best practices for CORS recommend setting the CORS-enabling Access-Control-Allow-Origin header only on pages where it is actually needed, rather than setting it globally on every page. Also consider the security implications of allowing CORS requests globally, particularly when using the wildcard "*".

You may also allow a single domain instead of allowing all domains with the wildcard. Until the CORS specification supporting multiple allowed domains is widely supported in client browsers, you will need to use additional logic in code to allow a specific set of allowed domains.

Setting CORS headers globally with web.config for IIS7 Server

Add this snippet in the web.config file at the root of your application. If you don't have a web.config file already, create a new file named web.config containing this code:

```xml
<?xml version="1.0" encoding="utf-8"?>
  <configuration>
    <system.webServer>
```

```
    <httpProtocol>
      <customHeaders>
        <add name="Access-Control-Allow-Origin" value="*" />
      </customHeaders>
    </httpProtocol>
  </system.webServer>
</configuration>
```

Setting CORS headers globally with IIS manager for IIS 8.5 and higher

In IIS6 server you can add the Access-Control-Allow-Origin header in IIS manager by completing the following steps:

1. Open the **Internet Information Service (IIS)** manager.

2. Expand the Sites folder.

3. Select the site where you want to enable CORS.

4. Double-click the HTTP Response Headers icon under the IIS category in the middle pane.

5. Under HTTP Response Headers, right-click and select the **Add** menu item.

6. For the header name, enter Access-Control-Allow-Origin in the **Name** field.

7. For the header value, enter a specific domain or the wildcard (*) in the **Value** field.

8. Click **Ok**.

CORS in the ASP.NET Web API

The ASP.NET Web API is a HTTP service-oriented framework suitable for implementing cross-domain requests via CORS in web applications.

> *ASP.NET Web API is a framework that makes it easy to build HTTP services that reach a broad range of clients, including browsers and mobile devices. ASP. NET Web API is an ideal platform for building RESTful applications on the .NET Framework.*

The EnableCorsAttribute custom class contains properties for the allowed origins, HTTP methods, request headers, response headers, and whether credentials are allowed.

The `CorsMessageHandler` checks the policy in the attribute for the `HTTP` method being invoked and sends the appropriate CORS response headers.

Enabling CORS in the ASP.NET Web API

When using the ASP.NET Web API, you may enable CORS globally on the IIS server using the methods already discussed.

It is preferable to add the CORS headers only on the pages, and for classes and methods, where they are needed. The next section shows how to fine-tune CORS policies in the Web API.

Installing the Web API Cross-Origin Support Package

Using the `NuGet` package manager for the Microsoft development platform, install the `Microsoft ASP.NET Web API Cross-Origin Support` package, by running the following command in the package manager console:

```
PM> Install-Package Microsoft.AspNet.WebApi.Cors
```

If you're not using `NuGet`, CORS is available as part of Visual Studio; reference two assemblies: `System.Web.Http.Cors.dll` and `System.Web.Cors.dll`.

There is also a `Cross-Origin Support` package available in `NuGet` when not using the Web API: .

However, if you are building a REST application with ASP.NET using CORS, the Web API is recommended because it has features designed for REST requests.

Enabling the CorsMessageHandler

The `CorsMessageHandler` must be enabled for the CORS framework to process requests, check the CORS policy, and send the CORS response headers. The message handler is typically enabled in the application's Web API configuration class by invoking the `EnableCors` extension method:

```
public static class WebApiConfig
{
  public static void Register(HttpConfiguration config)
  {
```

```
    // Other configurations omitted
    config.EnableCors();
  }
}
```

 The CorsMessageHandler can also be registered for each route rather than globally.

The EnableCorsAttribute class sets the CORS policies

The EnableCorsAttribute class can set the CORS policy for a method, a class, or globally.

The EnableCorsAttribute class constructor accepts the following parameters, which should look familiar from the CORS specification:

Required parameters for the EnableCorsAttribute class constructor:

- Allowed origins
- Allowed headers
- Allowed HTTP methods

Optional parameters for the EnableCorsAttribute class constructor:

- Allowed response headers
- SupportsCredentials (specifies if credentials are supported)
- PreflightMaxAge (specifies the preflight cache duration)

 Another attribute class named DisableCorsAttribute removes the policy for a method, class, or globally.

Configuring the EnableCors class attributes in the ASP.NET Web API

The `CorsMessageHandler` can be registered per-route rather than globally.

CORS policies can be set for specific HTTP methods.

Example: setting CORS policy for HTTP methods GET, PUT, and POST

This example defines CORS attributes for GET, PUT, and POST methods, one at a time:

```
public class ResourcesController : ApiController
{
  [EnableCors("http://www.localdomain.com",  // Origin making the
request
    null,          // no request headers allowed
    "GET",           // GET HTTP method
    "some response header",     // allowed response header
    SupportsCredentials=true    // Allow credentials
  )]
  // GET METHOD
  public HttpResponseMessage Get(int id)
  {
    var resp = Request.CreateResponse(HttpStatusCode.NoContent);
    resp.Headers.Add("some response header", "some response header
value");
    return resp;
  }
  // PUT METHOD
  [EnableCors("http://www.localdomain.com",  // Origin making the
request
    "Accept, Origin, Content-Type",  // Allowed request headers
    "PUT",  // PUT HTTP method
    PreflightMaxAge=600  // Preflight cache duration
  )]
  public HttpResponseMessage Put(Resource data)
  {
    return Request.CreateResponse(HttpStatusCode.OK, data);
  }
// POST METHOD
  [EnableCors("http://www.localdomain.com",  // Origin
    "Accept, Origin, Content-Type",    // Allowed request headers
    "POST",            // POST HTTP method
```

```
      PreflightMaxAge=600           // Preflight cache duration
   )]
   public HttpResponseMessage Post(Resource data)
   {
      return Request.CreateResponse(HttpStatusCode.OK, data);
   }
}
```

Use a "*" as the wildcard value to allow all origins, request headers, or HTTP methods. When response headers are allowed, the header(s) must always be given explicitly, as shown in the GET method.

In the following examples, the EnableCors class constructor is shown on one line, with the same nested structure as the previous example. The following code enables CORS from all origins, accepting all request headers, and allowing all HTTP methods:

```
[EnableCors("*", "*", "*")]s
```

Inheriting CORS Policy

The EnableCors policy can be set at the method level, at the class level, or globally. CORS policy applies for all requests inherited below the level where it is set. CORS policy set at the method level will only apply to requests under that method; CORS policy set at the class level will apply for all requests to that controller. CORS policy set globally will apply to all requests.

If there are policies at multiple levels, the precedence is from the most specific to the most general: method, then class, then global.

Setting CORS policy with wildcards

The policy set in these examples uses the wildcard "*", which is used for the allowed origins, request headers, and HTTP methods. This kind of permissiveness is not recommended because it can lead to security vulnerabilities. However, it may be necessary for some applications, at least temporarily; after all the requests are processed, a more restrictive policy may be set, or the CORS policy can be disabled with the DisableCors attribute.

Example: Setting CORS policy globally with wildcards

```
[EnableCors("*", "*", "*")]
public class ResourcesController : ApiController
{
   public HttpResponseMessage Put(Resource data)
   {
```

```
      return Request.CreateResponse(HttpStatusCode.OK, data);
   }
   public HttpResponseMessage Post(Resource data)
   {
      return Request.CreateResponse(HttpStatusCode.OK, data);
   }
}
```

Example: Setting a global CORS policy with the WebApiConfig class

An instance of the `EnableCorsAttribute` class can be passed as a parameter to the `EnableCors` method. The following code uses wildcards globally via the `WebApiConfig` class:

```
public static class WebApiConfig
{
   public static void Register(HttpConfiguration config)
   {
     // Other configurations omitted
     config.EnableCors(new EnableCorsAttribute("*", "*", "*"));
   }
}
```

Disallowing CORS in classes or methods

Since CORS policies are inherited, you may want to disallow CORS on specific classes or methods that inherit a policy:

*   Explicit values can be set in the allowed HTTP method(s) list
*   You can exclude a specific HTTP method with the `DisableCors` attribute

Example: Using explicit values for HTTP methods

This example allows PUT and POST HTTP methods, but GET and DELETE are not allowed:

```
[EnableCors("*", "*", "PUT, POST")]
public class ResourcesController : ApiController
{
   public HttpResponseMessage Put(Resource data)
   {
      return Request.CreateResponse(HttpStatusCode.OK, data);
   }
```

```
public HttpResponseMessage Post(Resource data)
{
   return Request.CreateResponse(HttpStatusCode.OK, data);
}
// CORS not allowed for DELETE because DELETE is not in the method
list
public HttpResponseMessage Delete(int id)
{
   return Request.CreateResponse(HttpStatusCode.NoContent);
}
}
```

Example: Using the DisableCors attribute

The DisableCors attribute disables a CORS policy and returns the HTTP status code for nocontent when a CORS request is made. In this example, CORS policy is enabled with wildcards, then disabled with DisableCors. Although it does not make sense to enable and immediately disable CORS, consider that in an actual application, some requests may be processed after CORS is enabled. CORS can be disabled when no longer needed:

```
[EnableCors("*", "*", "*")] // Enable CORS permissively
// Disable CORS for DELETE, as in the previous example:
public class ResourcesController : ApiController
{
   public HttpResponseMessage Put(Resource data)
   {
      return Request.CreateResponse(HttpStatusCode.OK, data);
   }
   public HttpResponseMessage Post(Resource data)
   {
      return Request.CreateResponse(HttpStatusCode.OK, data);
   }
   // CORS not allowed because of the [DisableCors] attribute
   [DisableCors]
   public HttpResponseMessage Delete(int id)
   {
      return Request.CreateResponse(HttpStatusCode.NoContent);
   }
}
```

Dynamic ASP.NET Web API CORS policies

We have looked at configuring CORS policies statically by providing fixed strings for the attribute values. When the list of allowed origins (or other attributes) needs to be determined dynamically, there are two options:

1. Custom CORS policy attribute class

    Creates a new CorsPolicy class with the `ICorsPolicyProvider` interface, and provides an implicit association from a request to a policy.

2. Custom CORS policy provider factory

    Creates a new CorsPolicy class with the `ICorsPolicyProviderFactory` interface IF the incoming request passes some logical test. This is the most flexible approach, but it may require more work to determine the policy from the request.

Custom CORS policy attribute classes

The `ICorsPolicyProvider` interface creates an instance of a CorsPolicy for any specified request. It can generate the policy from some data source, for example a database query. A custom attribute class can be used instead of the `EnableCorsAttribute` class provided by Web API. This simple approach can be applied to an attribute on specific classes and methods, and exclude others.

Example: A custom CORS policy class

This example builds a custom CORS attribute class with the custom `ICorsPolicyProvider` interface named `EnableCorsForPaidCustomersAttribute`, which is similar to the existing `EnableCorsAttribute` class. The constructor `var policy = new CorsPolicy` creates a new CorsPolicy that inherits all the necessary properties. The values could be provided dynamically from a database query, or from some other data source.

The custom `EnableCorsForPaidCustomersAttribute` class allows any header and method, but looks up allowed origins dynamically to match the request origin:

```
[AttributeUsage(AttributeTargets.Class | AttributeTargets.Method,
                AllowMultiple = false)]
public class EnableCorsForPaidCustomersAttribute :
  Attribute, ICorsPolicyProvider
{
```

```
public async Task<CorsPolicy> GetCorsPolicyAsync(
  HttpRequestMessage request, CancellationToken cancellationToken)
{
  var corsRequestContext = request.GetCorsRequestContext();
  var originRequested = corsRequestContext.Origin;
  if (await IsOriginFromAPaidCustomer(originRequested))
  {
    // Grant CORS request by constructing a new CorsPolicy
    var policy = new CorsPolicy
    {
      AllowAnyHeader = true,
      AllowAnyMethod = true,
    };
    policy.Origins.Add(originRequested);
    return policy;
  }
  else
  {
    // Reject CORS request
    return null;
  }
}
private async Task<bool> IsOriginFromAPaidCustomer(
  string originRequested)
{
  // Do database look up here; if the origin matches allow it with
return true
  return true;
}
}
```

Custom policy provider factory

The policy provider factory is part of the Web API CORS framework that gets the policy provider for the current request. By default, the Web API uses custom attribute values to determine the policy provider, with the attribute class itself as the policy provider. You can use the policy provider factory to create a custom CORS policy that requires more than custom attributes.

Using an attribute-based approach creates an implicit association from a request to a policy. A custom policy provider factory is different from using an attribute because it matches the incoming request to a policy. The policy provider factory is less specific, because it obtains the CORS policy from its central settings.

Registering the DynamicPolicyProviderFactory in WebApiConfig

To register the custom policy provider factory with Web API via the
`SetCorsPolicyProviderFactory` extension method:

```
public static class WebApiConfig
{
  public static void Register(HttpConfiguration config)
  {
    // Other configurations omitted
    config.EnableCors();
    config.SetCorsPolicyProviderFactory(
      new DynamicPolicyProviderFactory());
  }
}
```

Example: A custom CORS policy provider factory

The policy provider factory uses the `ICorsPolicyProviderFactory` interface and
its `GetCorsPolicyProvider` method. The route and controller for the factory are
defined. The factory dynamically determines if the controller is allowed for the origin
of the CORS request. If allowed, the policy provider factory creates a CorsPolicy with
the same constructor used in the custom CORS policy attribute class:

```
var policy = new CorsPolicy();
```

This example compares the CORS request origin with stored values in a database or
another data source. If the origin is allowed, it creates a custom CorsPolicy allowing
the HTTP method GET:

```
public class DynamicPolicyProviderFactory : ICorsPolicyProviderFactory
{
  public ICorsPolicyProvider GetCorsPolicyProvider(
    HttpRequestMessage request)
  {
    var route = request.GetRouteData();
    var controller = (string)route.Values["controller"];
    var corsRequestContext = request.GetCorsRequestContext();
    var originRequested = corsRequestContext.Origin;
    var policy = GetPolicyForControllerAndOrigin(
      controller, originRequested);
    return new CustomPolicyProvider(policy);
  }
```

```
  private CorsPolicy GetPolicyForControllerAndOrigin(
    string controller, string originRequested)
  {
    // Do database lookup to determine if the controller is allowed
for
    // the origin and create CorsPolicy if it is (otherwise return
null)
    var policy = new CorsPolicy();
    policy.Origins.Add(originRequested);
    policy.Methods.Add("GET");
    return policy;
  }
}
public class CustomPolicyProvider : ICorsPolicyProvider
{
  CorsPolicy policy;
  public CustomPolicyProvider(CorsPolicy policy)
  {
    this.policy = policy;
  }
  public Task<CorsPolicy> GetCorsPolicyAsync(
    HttpRequestMessage request, CancellationToken cancellationToken)
  {
    return Task.FromResult(this.policy);
  }
}
```

Debugging the ASP.NET Web API Cross-Origin support framework

You can find out why a particular XHR request isn't being granted permission by inspecting the CORS HTTP headers — or by checking if the headers are missing.

Server-side debugging

The Web API provides detailed trace messages using an ItraceWriter with information about the selected policy provider selected, the active policy, and the CORS HTTP headers.

Client-side debugging

You can use the browser's F12 developer tools to inspect an error message when an XHR CORS call fails.

Alternatively, inspect all HTTP requests with a HTTP debugger, such as `Fiddler`.

CORS in Windows Communication Foundation

Windows Communication Foundation (WCF) is another service-oriented Windows .NET framework component that is suitable for building applications that use CORS.

The WCF sends data as asynchronous messages from one service endpoint to another. A service endpoint can be hosted by IIS, or it can be hosted in an application. It can be a client of a service that requests data from a service endpoint.

Out of the box, WCF cannot make cross-origin requests because it does not send the required CORS headers: `Access-Control-Allow-Origin`, `Access-Control-Allow-Methods`, and `Access-Control-Allow-Methods`. WCF can also send the optional CORS headers: `Access-Control-Allow-Headers` and `Access-Control-Max-Age`.

Create a `global.asax` file to add the necessary HTTP headers to `Application_BeginRequest`. The following example of code for the `global.asax` file allows a request from `http://localdomain.com`, using allowed HTTP methods `POST`, `PUT`, `DELETE`. It allows `http://localdomain.com` to send the HTTP header "`Content-Type, Accept`" and it sets the TTL for the cached request to `1728000` seconds:

```
protected void Application_BeginRequest(object sender, EventArgs e)
{
    HttpContext.Current.Response.AddHeader("Access-Control-Allow-
Origin", "http://localdomain.com");
    if (HttpContext.Current.Request.HttpMethod == "OPTIONS")
    {
        HttpContext.Current.Response.AddHeader("Access-Control-Allow-
Methods", "POST, PUT, DELETE");

        HttpContext.Current.Response.AddHeader("Access-Control-Allow-
Headers", "Content-Type, Accept");
        HttpContext.Current.Response.AddHeader("Access-Control-Max-
Age", "1728000");
        HttpContext.Current.Response.End();
    }
}
```

Another potential way to iterate on settings quickly would be to move the `settings` dictionary out of the code into datafiles such as `json` or `yaml`. Then you can edit those files by hand or even build a quick editor.

Another approach is to add the custom CORS headers for the server in `Web.config` in the `system.webServer` section. Note that the discouraged wildcard "*" is used for security, so you should provide a single allowed domain, or use additional logic in code to allow multiple domains:

```
<httpProtocol>
  <customHeaders>
    <add name="Access-Control-Allow-Origin" value="*"/>
    <add name="Access-Control-Allow-Headers" value="Content-Type,
Accept" />
    <add name="Access-Control-Allow-Methods" value="POST,GET,OPTIONS"
/>
    <add name="Access-Control-Max-Age" value="1728000" />
  </customHeaders>
</httpProtocol>
```

 We recommend the first example because it modifies `Application_BeginRequest` where the requests are first handled in the application, rather than modifying the server in \ `Web.config`.

CORS in Windows browsers – Internet Explorer and Edge

The good news is that Edge, the browser that ships with Windows 10, and Internet Explorer 10 fully support the W3C specification for CORS, and you can use standard techniques with **XmlHttpRequest (XHR)** and CORS headers. Internet Explorer 7 and older versions do not support CORS at all.

According to Can I Use... (as of August 2015), CORS is supported by 97.69% of browsers in the USA and 92.76% globally. For more information about CORS support in browsers, see the Can I Use... page for CORS: .

In Internet Explorer 8 and 9, you have to use feature detection and XDomainRequest instead of XHR. We covered using XDomainRequest in *Chapter 1, Why You Need CORS*.

The following example shows how to detect XHR withCredentials and XDomainRequest support. If a new XmlHttpRequest has "withCredentials", then CORS is supported; if the window has XDomainRequest, then that method is supported; if neither is present, you cannot use CORS:

```
function browserSupportsCors() {
  if ("withCredentials" in new XmlHttpRequest())
    return true;
  else if (window.XDomainRequest)
    return true;
  else
    return false;
}
```

Summary

Interesting isn't it?

In this chapter, we have learned about how to allow incoming CORS requests in the Windows IIS server by adding the CORS headers in the web.config file.

Then we discussed how to use the REST features in the ASP.NET Web API framework to enable CORS.

Next, we learned about using CORS in the **Windows Communication Foundation (WCF)**.

Finally, we discussed CORS support in Edge and Internet Explorer 10 browsers.

6
CORS in the Cloud

We are now in a cloud computing era. Most applications and APIs are hosted in the cloud. Many SaaS applications offering their services are hosted in the cloud, enabling users to consume their APIs from their applications. We will discuss the following in this chapter:

- CORS in Amazon Simple Storage Service (S3)
- Using CORS in Google Cloud Storage
- Authenticated access to Google APIs with CORS
- CORS in IBM Cloudant
- CORS in Windows Azure Storage
- CORS in Box.com API
- CORS in Dropbox API

CORS requests in cloud APIs

Even if you're not already using cloud storage and services, you will have heard about them. Amazon S3, Google Cloud Storage, Windows Azure, and IBM Cloudant all provide secure and scalable access to files, data, and other assets. Google APIs provide access to Google Products such as Drive, Search, Gmail, Translate, Google Maps, and YouTube, all hosted in the cloud on Google's infrastructure. In addition to storing files in Google Drive, you may have file storage in Box and Dropbox.

All of the APIs for these services support cross-domain requests with CORS. Using CORS can simplify your application, making proxy forwarding unnecessary. Keep in mind that you can also implement CORS with custom code for cases when the APIs don't support some of these platforms; however, it's usually better to use API methods when they are suitable.

Although the APIs and methods may change over time, having a sound understanding of CORS will help you implement cross-domain requests regardless of the specific syntax used by a cloud API.

CORS in Amazon Simple Storage Service (S3)

Amazon Simple Storage Service (**Amazon S3**) provides developers and IT teams with secure, durable, highly-scalable object storage.

Scenarios for needing CORS in Amazon S3

* You are hosting a website in an Amazon S3 bucket named website. Browsers load the website endpoint, . You want to use JavaScript on the web pages that are stored in this bucket to be able to make authenticated GET and PUT requests against the same bucket by using Amazon S3's API endpoint for the bucket . The same origin policy in a browser would normally block JavaScript from allowing those requests, but with CORS you can configure your bucket to allow cross-origin requests from website.s3-website-us-east-1.amazonaws.com (as the local domain) to the endpoint (as the target domain).

* You want to host a web font on your S3 bucket. Browsers require a CORS preflight check for loading web fonts, so you would configure the bucket that is hosting the web font to allow your web application (as the local domain) to make the requests to the bucket with the font (as the target domain).

How to enable CORS on an S3 bucket

A CORSConfiguration CORSRule tag is an XML document with rules that identify the origins allowed to access your bucket, the operations (HTTP methods) allowed for each origin, and other operation-specific information. You can add up to 100 rules to the configuration. Add the XML document to the bucket as the CORS subresource.

Elements in an S3 CORSRule

The elements specified in an S3 CORSRule follow the CORS specification. The required elements are AllowedOrigin and AllowedMethod. The optional elements are AllowedHeader (required for preflight), MaxAgeSeconds, and ExposeHeader.

AllowedOrigin element (required)

Specify the origin(s) that you want to allow cross-domain requests from — the local domain(s). The origin string can contain at most one * wildcard character, such as http://*.localdomain.com, to allow sub-domains. You can optionally specify the wildcard "*" as the origin to enable cross-origin requests from all origins. Keep in mind that allowing requests from any domain has security implications. You can also specify the HTTPS protocol to enable only requests from an origin secured with SSL.

AllowedMethod element (required)

The CORSRule AllowedMethod element specifies the allowed HTTP method(s): GET, PUT, POST, DELETE, and HEAD.

AllowedHeader element (optional, required for preflight)

The AllowedHeader element specifies which HTTP headers are allowed in a preflight request through the Access-Control-Request-Headers header. According to the CORS specification, preflight is required unless making a simple GET request. Each header name in the Access-Control-Request-Headers header requested by the local domain must match a corresponding name in the rule. Amazon S3 will send back only the allowed headers in a response.

Each AllowedHeader name in the rule can contain, at most, one "*" wildcard character. For example, <AllowedHeader>x-amz-*</AllowedHeader> will allow all Amazon-specific headers, all of which begin with x-amz-.

MaxAgeSeconds element (optional)

The MaxAgeSeconds element specifies the time in seconds (TTL) that your browser can cache the response for a preflight request as identified by the resource, the HTTP method, and the origin.

ExposeHeader element (optional)

The `ExposeHeader` element identifies response headers that you want to be able to access from your application on the local domain.

 For a sample list of headers that can be used in requests to Amazon S3 via `AllowedHeader` and `ExposeHeader`, refer to the common request headers in the Amazon Simple Storage Service API Reference guide .

CORSConfiguration CORSRules with required elements

The following CORSConfiguration has three CORSRules using the required elements, including the `AllowedHeader` element needed for preflight:

- The first rule allows cross-origin `PUT`, `POST`, and `DELETE` requests from the `http://www.localdomain1.com` origin. The rule also allows all headers in a preflight `OPTIONS` request through the `Access-Control-Request-Headers` header. In response to any preflight `OPTIONS` request, Amazon S3 will return any requested headers.

- The second rule allows the same cross-origin requests as in the first rule, but the rule applies to another origin, `https://www.localdomain2.com`, using the https protocol over SSL. `http://www.localdomain2.com` without SSL would not be allowed.

- The third rule allows cross-origin `GET` requests from all origins. The `*` wildcard character refers to all origins. Since it is a simple `GET` request, preflight and the `AllowedHeader` element are not needed.

```
<CORSConfiguration>
 <CORSRule>
  <AllowedOrigin>http://www.localdomain1.com</AllowedOrigin>
  <AllowedMethod>PUT</AllowedMethod>
  <AllowedMethod>POST</AllowedMethod>
  <AllowedMethod>DELETE</AllowedMethod>
  <AllowedHeader>*</AllowedHeader>
 </CORSRule>
 <CORSRule>
  <AllowedOrigin>https://www.localdomain2.com</AllowedOrigin>
  <AllowedMethod>PUT</AllowedMethod>
  <AllowedMethod>POST</AllowedMethod>
```

```
    <AllowedMethod>DELETE</AllowedMethod>
    <AllowedHeader>*</AllowedHeader>
  </CORSRule>
  <CORSRule>
    <AllowedOrigin>*</AllowedOrigin>
    <AllowedMethod>GET</AllowedMethod>
  </CORSRule>
</CORSConfiguration>
```

CORSConfiguration CORSRule with optional elements

The following CORSConfiguration CORSRule includes optional elements. The MaxAgeSeconds value is set to cache the preflight request for 3000 seconds. The ExposeHeader values allow the Amazon response headers: x-amz-server-side-encryption, x-amz-request-id, and x-amz-id-2:

```
<CORSConfiguration>
  <CORSRule>
    <AllowedOrigin>http://www.localdomain.com</AllowedOrigin>
    <AllowedMethod>PUT</AllowedMethod>
    <AllowedMethod>POST</AllowedMethod>
    <AllowedMethod>DELETE</AllowedMethod>
    <AllowedHeader>*</AllowedHeader>
  <MaxAgeSeconds>3000</MaxAgeSeconds>
  <ExposeHeader>x-amz-server-side-encryption</ExposeHeader>
  <ExposeHeader>x-amz-request-id</ExposeHeader>
  <ExposeHeader>x-amz-id-2</ExposeHeader>
  </CORSRule>
</CORSConfiguration>
```

How does Amazon S3 evaluate the CORS Configuration on a bucket?

When Amazon S3 receives a preflight request from a browser, it evaluates the CORS configuration for the bucket and uses the first CORSRule rule that matches the incoming browser request to enable a cross-origin request. The following conditions must be met within a single CORSRule:

- The request's origin header must match an AllowedOrigin element

- The request HTTP method (for example, GET or PUT), or the Access-Control-Request-Method header in the case of a preflight OPTIONS request, must be one of the AllowedMethod elements

- Every header listed in the request's Access-Control-Request-Headers header on the preflight request must match an AllowedHeader element in the rule

 The ACLs and policies for the bucket continue to apply when you enable CORS on the bucket.

Using CORS in Google Cloud Storage

Google Cloud Storage stores your data on Google's infrastructure with very high reliability, performance, and availability. You can use Google Cloud Storage to distribute large data objects to users via direct download.

 Another potential way to iterate on settings quickly would be to move the settings dictionary out of the code into data files such as json or yaml. Then you can edit those files by hand or even build a quick editor.

Configuring CORS on a bucket in Google Cloud Storage

Google Cloud Storage allows you to set CORS configuration at the bucket-level only. A CORS configuration on the bucket contains all the allowed origins and request methods.

There are multiple ways to set the CORS configuration on a bucket:

- The gsutil cors set command gets, sets, or modifies CORS configuration.

- Send a request directly to the Google Cloud Storage XML API or JSON API. For example, you can use the PUT bucket method in the XML API, with the ?cors subresource in the URL to set or modify CORS configuration. Use the GET bucket with the ?cors subresource to list a bucket's CORS configuration.

- Use one of the client libraries for Google Cloud Storage.

Using gsutil cors set in Google Cloud Storage

The following `gsutil cors set` command applies configuration from the `cors-json-file.json` file on the bucket named `target`. The settings for `origin`, `responseHeader`, and HTTP methods follow the CORS specification. The `maxAgeSeconds` specifies the time to cache the preflight request:

```
gsutil cors set cors-json-file.json gs://target
```

The `cors-json-file.json` file contains the following:

```
[
  {
    "origin": ["http://localdomain.com"],
    "responseHeader": ["Content-Type"],
    "method": ["GET", "HEAD", "DELETE"],
    "maxAgeSeconds": 3600
  }
]
```

Using the XML API in Google Cloud Storage

The Google Cloud XML API provides a method to get or set a CORS configuration on a bucket via a request with the URL token ?cors.

You can specify the bucket name after the domain `storage.googleapis.com` and before the object-name, separated with slashes. You can also specify the bucket name as part of the hostname. If you are specifying the bucket as part of the hostname, then do not include the bucket name as part of the URI path. The following are its equivalents:

```
https://storage.googleapis.com/BUCKET-NAME/object-name?cors
```

```
https://BUCKET-NAME.storage.googleapis.com/object-name?cors
```

In the following examples, we will use the shorthand `[storage-url]`, which may be replaced by either URL syntax.

 Prior to sending a request, authentication must be established using the Google Cloud ACL request. For more information see: .

Getting CORS configuration for a bucket with the XML API

Use a GET request to retrieve the CORS configuration on a bucket. The GET request does not require an XML document:

```
GET [storage-url]?cors
```

Putting a CORSConfig on a bucket with the XML API

Use a PUT request to set or modify the CORS configuration on a bucket:

```
PUT [storage-url]?cors
```

The PUT request requires a CorsConfig XML document that provides the CORS parameters, which follow the CORS specification:

```
<CorsConfig>
 <Cors>
  <Origins>
   <Origin>http://localdomain.com</Origin>
  </Origins>
  <Methods>
   <Method>GET</Method>
   <Method>HEAD</Method>
   <Method>DELETE</Method>
  </Methods>
  <ResponseHeaders>
   <ResponseHeader>Content-Type</ResponseHeader>
  </ResponseHeaders>
  <MaxAgeSec>3600</MaxAgeSec>
 </Cors>
</CorsConfig>
```

Troubleshooting CORS-related problems in Google Cloud Storage

First, inspect the CORS configuration and the headers:

1. Use gsutil cors get on the problem bucket to ensure the bucket has the expected CORS configuration.

2. Capture a full request-response using a tool of your choice, for example, Chrome's browser developer tools.

Problems with headers

Ensure that the request actually has an origin header.

Ensure that the origin header you're sending matches at least one of the origin headers in the CORS configuration. Note that the scheme, host, and port must all match, per the same origin policy specification.

Ensure that the method you're sending (or the method specified in Access-Control-Request-Method, if this is a preflight request) is a match for one of the methods in your CORS configuration, that also is a match for origin. A CORS configuration entry must match on both origin and method.

If you have two CORS configuration entries, one of which matches on origin but not method, and the other matches on method but not origin, neither one will be used, and no CORS headers will be included in the response.

If this is a preflight request, check if the preflight request includes one or more Access-Control-Request-Header. Then, ensure that the matching CORS configuration entry includes a ResponseHeader entry for each requested header. All headers named in the Access-Control-Request-Header must be in the CORS configuration for the preflight request to succeed and include CORS headers in the response.

Problems with cached preflight requests

If you are trying to reproduce the problem, and you're not seeing a request/response, it is possible that your browser has cached an earlier failed preflight request attempt. Clearing your browser's cache may also clear the preflight cache.

The default setting for MaxAgeSec is 1800 seconds (30 minutes). If you think clearing your browser's cache in the usual way is also not clearing the CORS preflight cache, you should set MaxAgeSec on your CORS configuration to a lower value, wait 30 minutes, and then try again. This should perform a new preflight request, which will fetch the new CORS configuration and also set MaxAgeSec to the new lower value, allowing the cache entries to be purged more frequently. Once you have debugged your problem, you should raise MaxAgeSec back to a higher value, to reduce the preflight traffic to your bucket.

Problems with the resumable upload protocol

When using the resumable upload protocol, the origin from the first (start upload) request is always used to decide the `Access-Control-Allow-Origin` header in the response. If the first request has a different origin to subsequent requests, use the XML API with the `CORS` configuration set to `<Origin>*</Origin>` prior to starting the first request.

Authenticated access to Google APIs with CORS

Google APIs allow communication with Google Services, such as Drive, Search, Gmail, Translate, Google Maps, YouTube, and many others. You can leverage these APIs in a third-party application to take advantage of or extend the functionality of the existing Google Services.

The `Google API Client` library for JavaScript makes it easier for you to write JavaScript that works with Google Services.

Google APIs support **Cross-Origin Resource Sharing (CORS)**.

If you want your application to access a Google Service user's personal information, OAuth 2.0 provides authenticated access to the user's information.

For more information about the `Google API Client` Library for JavaScript see: .

OAuth and CORS are implemented via the `Google API Client` Library for JavaScript. Google also provides a standalone JavaScript auth client, which can be used without loading the entire JS library.

Google API Keys

Google defines two levels of API access:

- Simple API calls that do not access any private user data require a Google API key

- Authorized API calls can read and write private user data, or the Google application's own data, and require the Google API key plus OAuth 2.0 credentials

Register your application in the Google APIs console. For simple access, Google generates an API key that uniquely identifies your application in its transactions with the Google Auth server. For authorized access, you must also tell Google your website's protocol and domain. In return, Google generates a client ID. Your application submits the client ID to the Google Auth server to get an OAuth 2.0 access token.

Adding the Google API client library for JavaScript

The library may be added via a script tag. In this example, the `callback` function `OnLoadCallback` is executed when the library completes loading:

```
<script src="https://apis.google.com/js/client.
js?onload=OnLoadCallback"></script>
```

The Google API CORS request

A CORS request to the Google API uses `XmlHttpRequest2` (`XHR`). A Google API CORS request always includes the Google APIs domain, , followed by the path to the Google Service and the request query parameters as arguments. The request is executed by the `XHR` `send()` method.

Here is a simple `GET` request to Google+ (-encoded as `Google%2B`) to retrieve `activities` ordered by `best`:

```
var xhr = new XMLHttpRequest();
xhr.open('GET', 'https://www.googleapis.com/plus/v1/activities?query=G
oogle%2B&orderBy=best');
xhr.send();
```

The path to the Google+ "activities" service is `/plus/v1/activities`.

The request query parameters are `?query=Google%2B&orderBy=best`.

The preceding request without authentication via OAuth with the Google API will get an error message such as "Daily Limit for Unauthenticated Use Exceeded. Continued use requires signup." In the following section, we will see how to authenticate a request with Oauth.

Authenticated CORS requests to Google APIs with OAuth

Before you can make an authenticated CORS request, your application must send its Google API key, receive a client ID, and obtain an access token for making authenticated requests, by either using the `gapi.auth` methods from the `Google API Client` Library for JavaScript, or by using Google APIs' standalone auth client.

There are two ways to make an authenticated request with CORS:

1. Send the access token in the `Authorization request` header.

2. Include the access token as the `access_token` parameter in the URL.

There are two ways to retrieve an access token using the `Google API Client` Library for JavaScript:

1. It is provided as the first parameter to the `gapi.auth.authorize` callback.

2. It is also saved and can be accessed at any time by calling `gapi.auth.getToken`.

Example using the Authorization request header

Create a new XHR request and get the OAuth token. Set the HTTP method to `GET` and set the request URL. Then, with `xhr.setRequestHeader`, set the value of the `Authorization` header to `'Bearer ' + oauthToken.access_token`. Then, send the request:

```
var xhr = new XMLHttpRequest();
var oauthToken = gapi.auth.getToken();
xhr.open('GET',
 'https://www.googleapis.com/plus/v1/people/me/activities/public');
xhr.setRequestHeader('Authorization',
  'Bearer ' + oauthToken.access_token);
xhr.send();
```

Example using the access_token in the URL parameter

```
var xhr = new XMLHttpRequest();
var oauthToken = gapi.auth.getToken();
xhr.open('GET',
 'https://www.googleapis.com/plus/v1/people/me/activities/public' +
 '?access_token=' + encodeURIComponent(oauthToken.access_token));
xhr.send();
```

Here is a YouTube video about Google Drive SDK: CORS support: .

CORS in IBM Cloudant

IBM Cloudant is a NoSQL JSON document store that is optimized for handling heavy workloads of concurrent reads and writes in the cloud; a workload that is typical of large, fast-growing web and mobile apps. It provides a simple JSON API for configuring CORS for your database, which may be changed dynamically.

How to GET or PUT a CORS configuration in IBM Cloudant

IBM Cloudant provides the endpoint `/_api/v2/user/config/cors`. A GET call to the endpoint retrieves the CORS configuration for your application. You can change the CORS configuration with a PUT call to the endpoint.

How to GET a CORS Configuration

The following request reads the CORS configuration. Note that both `localdomain.com` and `www.localdomain.com` are allowed origins, since they are considered different domains under the same origin policy. This example also allows requests only from domains on HTTPS secured with SSL; you may allow a domain over HTTP, understanding the risk:

```
GET /_api/v2/user/config/cors HTTP/1.1
Host: username.cloudant.com
```

The response looks as follows:

```
HTTP/1.1 200 OK
Content-Type: application/json
Content-Length: 178
{
  "enable_cors": true,
  "allow_credentials": true,
  "origins": [
    "https://localdomain.com",
    "https://www.localdomain.com"
  ]
}
```

Set or Modify a CORS Configuration

Use a PUT request to set or modify a CORS configuration:

```
PUT /_api/v2/user/config/cors HTTP/1.1
Host: $USERNAME.cloudant.com
Content-Type: application/json
{
  "enable_cors": true,
  "allow_credentials": true,
  "origins": [
     "https://localdomain.com",
     "https://www.localdomain.com"
   ]
}
```

A successful response would return the following:

```
{ "ok": true }
```

Security considerations when CORS in IBM Cloudant

IBM Cloudant documentation provides recommendations for sensible CORS security, such as:

- Allow CORS requests only from HTTPS origins secured with SSL

- Ensure that web applications running on allowed origin domains are trusted and do not have security vulnerabilities

- Don't allow CORS requests from all origins with the wildcard * unless you are certain that:

  1. You want to allow all data in your databases to be publicly accessible.
  2. User credentials that give permission to modify data are never used in a browser.

IBM Cloudant also supports CORS and reverse proxies in Node.js/Express, which will be covered in the chapter about Node.js.

CORS in Windows Azure Storage

Without CORS, all cross-domain requests to the Windows Azure Storage service would need to be proxied via the service, and the service would have to scale the proxy servers for an increased load. As we have seen already, CORS removes the need for an intermediate proxy for cross-domain requests.

CORS is supported for the Blob, Table, and Queue services in Azure, and can be enabled for each service through the Windows Azure Storage Client Library.

 More details about CORS for Windows Azure Storage are available in an MSDN blog post: .

CORS usage scenarios for Windows Azure Storage

The following are some scenarios explaining why CORS may be used for Blobs and Tables in Windows Azure:

CORS for Windows Azure Blobs (file uploads)

CORS for Blobs allows direct file uploads to a Windows Azure Storage account through the client browser. CORS, along with the **Shared Access Signature (SAS)** authentication mechanism, grant the user write privileges to your storage account in the client browser. Whenever a user is ready to upload, JavaScript code would request a blob SAS URL for the upload from your service and then perform a PUT Blob request.

 It is recommended that you limit the access time of the SAS token for the anticipated time needed to upload the file, in order to limit any security risks.

CORS for Windows Azure Table

CORS for Windows Azure Table can display table data, and allow the manipulation of table data in the browser. For example, you can use CORS, SAS, JSON, and jQuery to expose an administration page where a user can change the configuration settings for your website that you persist in a Windows Azure Table.

Preflight requests in Windows Azure

Preflight requests are required by the Azure service. The preflight request is an OPTIONS request that carries the actual request headers, including the type of HTTP request and the origin domain. The Azure service evaluates the OPTIONS based on a preconfigured set of rules that allow origin domains, types of requested headers, methods, and so on, and the request is accepted if it matches a rule. In Windows Azure Storage, CORS rules are configured per service (Blob, Table, or Queue) and the preflight requests are evaluated per service.

Preflight requests are typically cached by the browser and subsequent requests can skip the preflight during the cache period set by the TTL value.

Code examples for CORS in Windows Azure

CORS in Windows Azure requires you to configure rules, which can be defined statically when configuring a Windows Azure Service, or they may be defined and applied dynamically in code.

Static CORS rules in Windows Azure

You can configure up to five CORS rules for each storage service (that is, Blob, Table, or Queue). The metadata follows the CORS specification, defining Allowed Origins (note that you can allow more than one specific domain) and methods. The Allowed Headers and Exposed Headers are specific to the Azure framework.

The MaxAgeInSeconds indicates the maximum amount of time that a browser can cache the preflight OPTIONS request.

 MaxAgeInSeconds should be set to a relatively large number if the rules do not change frequently, since this will increase the responsiveness of your web application by reducing roundtrips, and will also reduce your storage billing charges as preflight requests are billed.

A single CORS rule is defined as follows:

```
<CorsRule>
  <AllowedOrigins>http://www.contoso.com, http://www.fabrikam.com</
AllowedOrigins>
  <AllowedMethods>PUT,GET</AllowedMethods>
```

```
 <AllowedHeaders>x-ms-meta-data*,x-ms-meta-target,x-ms-meta-source</
AllowedHeaders>
 <ExposedHeaders>x-ms-meta-*</ExposedHeaders>
 <MaxAgeInSeconds>200</MaxAgeInSeconds>
</CorsRule>
```

> CORS rules are evaluated in the order they appear in XML as part of the Set Service Properties REST API. The more restrictive rules defining specific allowed domains should be set first. Any rule using the wildcard "*" should come last. Details about CORS rule evaluation are explained in the Understanding CORS Rule Evaluation Logic MSDN documentation: .

Dynamically configuring CORS in Windows Azure

It's also possible to configure CORS rules dynamically in code. These code snippets are from the MSDN Windows Azure Storage CORS Sample: .

Enabling CORS on a Windows Azure Storage account for the blob (file) service

This example gets the current service properties, enables CORS with a single rule allowing all origins and HTTP methods (PUT, GET, HEAD, and POST), and then commits the modified service properties for both the Blob and Table Services:

```
private static void InitializeCors()
{
    // CORS should be enabled once at service startup
    // Get the current Service Properties for Blob and Table
    ServiceProperties blobServiceProperties = BlobClient.
GetServiceProperties();
    ServiceProperties tableServiceProperties = TableClient.
GetServiceProperties();

    // Enable and Configure CORS
    ConfigureCors(blobServiceProperties);
    ConfigureCors(tableServiceProperties);

    // Commit the CORS changes for the Blob and Table Service
Properties
```

```
    BlobClient.SetServiceProperties(blobServiceProperties);
    TableClient.SetServiceProperties(tableServiceProperties);
}

private static void ConfigureCors(ServiceProperties serviceProperties)
{
    serviceProperties.Cors = new CorsProperties();
    serviceProperties.Cors.CorsRules.Add(new CorsRule()
    {
      AllowedHeaders = new List<string>() { "*" },
      AllowedMethods = CorsHttpMethods.Put | CorsHttpMethods.Get |
CorsHttpMethods.Head | CorsHttpMethods.Post,
      AllowedOrigins = new List<string>() { "*" },
      ExposedHeaders = new List<string>() { "*" },
      MaxAgeInSeconds = 1800
    });
}
```

JavaScript code for uploading an image to a Windows Azure Storage Blob service with CORS in ASP.NET

This ASP.NET code snippet uploads a file (Blob) directly from the browser into Windows Azure Storage using JavaScript. The code passes the `Blob SAS URL` and `fileDataAsArrayBuffer` (raw file data) from the ASP.NET application, then uploads the image into Azure Storage, or displays an error message if the upload fails. After the image is successfully uploaded, it calls `renderImage` to display the uploaded image. The client browser adds the necessary CORS headers defined in the blob service, and issues the preflight request. Note that the blob service must have allowed access from the domain in the `Blob SAS URL`, and the `PUT` method, in a CORS rule:

```
function uploadImage(blobSasUrl, fileDataAsArrayBuffer) {
    var ajaxRequest = new XMLHttpRequest();
    ajaxRequest.onreadystatechange = function() {return
renderImage(ajaxRequest, blobSasUrl)};

    try {
      // Put the Blob into storage
      ajaxRequest.open('PUT', blobSasUrl, true);
      ajaxRequest.setRequestHeader('Content-Type', 'image/jpeg');
      ajaxRequest.setRequestHeader('x-ms-blob-type', 'BlockBlob');
      ajaxRequest.send(fileDataAsArrayBuffer);
```

```
  }
  catch (e) {
    alert("can't upload the image to server.\n" + e.toString());
  }
}
```

CORS on a Windows Azure Storage account for the table service

The MSDN blog post introducing CORS in Azure referenced previously also includes jQuery code for accessing Windows Azure Tables. A starting point would be the `InsertTableEntities.cshtml` and `QueryTableEntities.cshtml` example files.

CORS in Box API

Box provides simple storage of files, which may be shared via `view/download` links. The Box API supports CORS on an app-by-app basis. Contact the Box team with a description of your use case so that they can allow access from your local domain when making the CORS request. They provide an example of an Ajax upload using jQuery:

```
// Set up the multipart form using HTML5 FormData object
var form = new FormData();

// The content of the file
// The file content could be read via jQuery.get()
var fileBody = '<p>hey!<p>';

// JS file-like object
var blob = new Blob([fileBody], { type: 'text/xml'});

// Add the file to the form
form.append('file', blob);

// Add the destination folder for the upload to the form
form.append('parent_id', '0');

var uploadUrl = 'https://upload.box.com/api/2.0/files/content';

// The Box OAuth 2 Header. Add your access token.
var headers = {
```

```
    Authorization: 'Bearer YOUR_ACCESS_TOKEN' // your Box API Access
Token
};

$.ajax({
  url: uploadUrl,
  headers: headers,     // the CORS HTTP headers
  type: 'POST',     // the CORS HTTP method
  // This prevents jQuery from trying to append the form as a
querystring
  processData: false,
  contentType: false,
  data: form
}).complete(function ( data ) {
  // Log the JSON response
  console.log(data.responseText);
});
```

CORS in the Dropbox API

Dropbox provides the simple storage of files, which may be shared via preview/
download links. CORS is supported for direct links in the Dropbox chooser, which
allows you to read the file information directly in the browser using client-side
JavaScript. Direct links should not be used to display content directly in the browser.
Direct links point directly to the contents of the file and are useful for downloading
the file itself. Unlike Preview Links, they expire after four hours, so make sure to
download the contents of the file immediately after the file is chosen.

Refer to the Dropbox documentation for more information on using chooser: .

Support for simple requests using simple headers via CORS, including support for
XdomainRequest, is provided in dropbox.js in the src/util/xhr.coffee file.
dropbox.js is the unofficial JavaScript library for the Dropbox core API:

```
# Using the header names listed at
# http://www.w3.org/TR/cors/#simple-response-header
# and the names used by the Dropbox API server in
# access-control-expose-headers.
for name in ['cache-control', 'content-language', 'content-range',
        'content-type', 'expires', 'last-modified', 'pragma',
        'x-dropbox-metadata']
```

```
  value = @xhr.getResponseHeader name
  headers[name] = value if value
headers


# Handles the XDomainRequest onload event. (IE 8, 9)
onXdrLoad: ->
# WebKit fires onreadystatechange multiple times, might as well
include the
# same fix in IE-specific code.
 return true if @completed
 @completed = true
 text = @xhr.responseText
```

dropbox.js is hosted on GitHub: .

There is also a middleware library CORS 1.0.0 by 3scale hosted on GitHub that allows you to use the Dropbox API directly from the browser .

Summary

We have learnt how to apply CORS in various services across the web. Let us recollect each one of them. We started with an understanding of how to use CORS with Amazon S3, Google Cloud Storage, and Windows Azure.

Then, we learned about how to use CORS in the `Google API Client` library for JavaScript to interact with Google products and services. We also discussed how to use CORS with IBM Cloudant's data storage service.

Finally, we discussed how to use CORS so that it interacts with files stored in Box and Dropbox. To interact with Google Drive files, use the `Google API Client` library for JavaScript or the Google Drive SDK.

References

Amazon S3 "Enabling Cross-Origin Resource Sharing" documentation .

7
CORS in Node.js

Node.js is a cross-platform JavaScript runtime environment that executes JavaScript code at the server-side. This enables a unified language across the web application development. JavaScript becomes the unified language that runs both on the client-side and server-side.

In this chapter, we will learn about the following topics:

- Node.js as a JavaScript platform for developing server-side web applications

- Node.js can provide the web server for other frameworks, including Express.js, AngularJS, Backbone.js, Ember.js, and others

- Other JavaScript frameworks, such as ReactJS, Ember.js, and Socket.IO, may also use Node.js as the web server

- Isomorphic JavaScript can add server-side functionality for client-side frameworks

- JavaScript frameworks are evolving rapidly; this chapter reviews some of the current techniques and specific syntax for some of these frameworks, so make sure that you check the documentation of the project to discover the latest techniques

- Through understanding CORS concepts, you will be able to create your own solution, because JavaScript is a loosely-structured language

- All examples are based on the fundamentals of CORS, with allowed origin(s), methods, and headers, such as `Content-Type`, or `preflight`, which may be required according to the CORS specification

JavaScript frameworks are very popular

JavaScript is sometimes called the lingua franca of the Internet, because it is cross-platform and supported by many devices. It is also a loosely-structured language, which makes it possible for users to craft solutions for many types of applications.

Sometimes an entire application is built in JavaScript. Frequently, JavaScript provides a client-side frontend for applications built with Symfony, content management systems, such as Drupal, and other backend frameworks.

Node.js is server-side JavaScript, and provides a web server as an alternative to Apache, IIS, Nginx, and other traditional web servers.

Introduction to Node.js

Node.js is an open-source and cross-platform library that is enabled when developing server-side web applications. Applications written using JavaScript in Node.js can run on many operating systems, including OS X, Microsoft Windows, Linux, and many others. Node.js provides a non-blocking I/O and an event-driven architecture designed to optimize an application's performance and scalability for real-time web applications. The biggest difference between PHP and Node.js is that PHP is a blocking language, where commands execute only after the previous command has completed, while Node.js is a non-blocking language, where commands execute in parallel, and callbacks are used to signal completion. Node.js can move files, payloads from services, and data asynchronously, without waiting for some command to complete, which improves performance.

Most JS frameworks that work with Node.js use the concept of routes to manage pages and other parts of the application. Each route may have its own set of configurations. For example, CORS may be enabled only for a specific page or route.

Node.js loads modules for extending functionality via the npm package manager. The developer selects which packages to load with npm, which reduces bloat. The developer community has created a large number of npm packages for specific functions.

JXcore is a fork of Node.js, targeting mobile devices and Internet of Things (IoT) devices. JXcore can use both Google V8 and Mozilla SpiderMonkey as its JavaScript engine. JXcore can run Node applications on iOS devices using Mozilla SpiderMonkey.

MEAN is a popular JavaScript software stack with MongoDB (a NoSQL database), Express.js, and AngularJS, all of which run on a Node.js server.

JavaScript frameworks that work with Node.js

Node.js provides a server for other popular JS frameworks, including AngularJS, Express.js. Backbone.js, Socket.IO, and Connect.js. ReactJS was designed to run in the client browser, but it is often combined with a Node.js server.

As we shall see in the following descriptions, these frameworks are not necessarily exclusive, and are often combined in applications.

Express.js is a Node.js server framework

Express.js is a Node.js web application server framework, designed for building single-page, multi-page, and hybrid web applications. It is considered the "standard" server framework for Node.js. The package is installed with the command `npm install express -save`.

AngularJS extends static HTML with dynamic views

HTML was designed for static content, not for dynamic views. AngularJS extends HTML syntax with custom tag attributes. It provides **model–view–controller (MVC)** and **model–view–viewmodel (MVVM)** architectures in a frontend, client-side framework. AngularJS is often combined with a Node.js server and other JS frameworks.

 AngularJS runs client-side and Express.js runs on the server, therefore Express.js is considered more secure for functions such as validating user input, which can be tampered with client-side. AngularJS applications can use the Express.js framework to connect to databases, for example in the MEAN stack.

Connect.js provides middleware for Node.js requests

Connect.js is a JavaScript framework providing middleware for handling requests in Node.js applications. Connect.js provides middleware to handle Express.js and cookie sessions, to provide parsers for the HTML body and cookies, and to create vhosts (virtual hosts) and error handlers, and to override methods.

Backbone.js often uses a Node.js server

Backbone.js is a JavaScript framework with a RESTful JSON interface, and is based on the **model–view–presenter** (**MVP**) application design. It is designed for developing single-page web applications, and for keeping various parts of web applications (for example, multiple clients and the server) synchronized. Backbone depends on Underscore.js and jQuery for the use of all the available features. Backbone often uses a Node.js server, for example, to connect to data storage.

ReactJS handles user interfaces

ReactJS is a JavaScript library for creating user interfaces while addressing challenges encountered in developing single-page applications where data changes over time. React handles the user interface in **model–view–controller** (**MVC**) architecture. ReactJS typically runs client-side and can be combined with AngularJS.

Although ReactJS was designed to run client-side, it can also be used server-side in conjunction with Node.js. PayPal and Netflix to leverage the server-side rendering of ReactJS, known as isomorphic ReactJS. There are also React-based add-ons that take care of the server-side parts of a web application.

Socket.IO uses WebSockets for real-time, event-driven applications

Socket.IO is a JavaScript library for event-driven web applications using the WebSocket protocol, with real-time, bi-directional communication between web clients and servers. It has two parts: a `client-side` library that runs in the browser, and a `server-side` library for Node.js. Although it can be used simply as a wrapper for WebSocket, it provides many more features, including broadcasting to multiple sockets, storing data associated with each client, and asynchronous I/O. Socket. IO provides better security than WebSocket alone, since allowed domains must be specified for its server.

Ember.js can use Node.js

Ember is another popular JavaScript framework with routing that uses `Moustache` templates. It can run on a Node.js server, or with Express.js. Ember can also be combined with Rack, a component of **Ruby on Rails** (**ROR**). We will examine CORS in Rack in the next chapter. Ember data is a library for modeling data in Ember.js applications.

CORS in Express.js

The following code adds the `Access-Control-Allow-Origin` and `Access-Control-Allow-Headers` headers globally to all requests on all routes in an Express.js application. A `route` is a path in the Express.js application, for example, `/user` for a user page. `app.all` sets the configuration for all routes in the application. Specific HTTP requests such as GET or POST are handled by `app.get` and `app.post`:

```
app.all('*', function(req, res, next) {
  res.header("Access-Control-Allow-Origin", "*");
  res.header("Access-Control-Allow-Headers", "X-Requested-With");
  next();
});

app.get('/', function(req, res, next) {
  // Handle GET for this route
});

app.post('/', function(req, res, next) {
// Handle the POST for this route
});
```

For better security, consider limiting the allowed origin to a single domain, or adding some additional code to validate or limit the domain(s) that are allowed. Also, consider limiting sending the headers only to routes that require CORS by replacing `app.all` with a more specific route and method.

The following code only sends the CORS headers on a GET request to the route `/user`, and only allows the request from `http://www.localdomain.com`:

```
app.get('/user', function(req, res, next) {
  res.header("Access-Control-Allow-Origin", "http://www.localdomain.
com");
  res.header("Access-Control-Allow-Headers", "X-Requested-With");
  next();
});
```

 Since this is JavaScript code, you may dynamically manage the values of routes, methods, and domains via variables, instead of hard-coding the values.

CORS npm for Express.js using Connect.js middleware

Connect.js provides middleware for handling requests in Express.js.

You can use **node package manager (npm)** to install a package that enables CORS in Express.js with Connect.js:

```
npm install cors
```

The package offers flexible options, which should be familiar to the CORS specification, including using credentials and preflight. It provides dynamic ways of validating an origin domain using a function or a regular expression, and handler functions to process preflight.

Configuration options for CORS npm

The following are the options for CORS npm:

origin: Configures the Access-Control-Allow-Origin CORS header with a string containing the full URL and protocol making the request, for example http://localdomain.com.

Possible values for origin:

- The default value TRUE uses req.header('Origin') to determine the origin and CORS is enabled
- When set to FALSE, CORS is disabled
- It can be set to a function with the request origin as the first parameter and a callback function as the second parameter
- It can be a regular expression, for example, /localdomain\.com$/, or an array of regular expressions and/or strings to match

methods: Sets the Access-Control-Allow-Methods CORS header.

Possible values for methods:

- A comma-delimited string of HTTP methods, for example 'GET,POST'
- An array of HTTP methods, for example ['GET', 'PUT', 'POST']

allowedHeaders: Sets the Access-Control-Allow-Headers CORS header.

Possible values for `allowedHeaders`:

- A comma-delimited string of allowed headers, for example `Content-Type,Authorization`
- An array of allowed headers, for example `['Content-Type', 'Authorization']`
- If unspecified, it defaults to the value specified in the request's `Access-Control-Request-Headers` header

`exposedHeaders`: Sets the `Access-Control-Expose-Headers` header.

Possible values for `exposedHeaders`:

- A comma-delimited string of exposed headers, for example `'Content-Range,X-Content-Range'`
- An array of exposed headers, for example `['Content-Range', 'X-Content-Range']`
- If unspecified, no custom headers are exposed

`credentials`: Sets the `Access-Control-Allow-Credentials` CORS header.

Possible values for `credentials`:

- `TRUE` — passes the header for `preflight`
- `FALSE` or unspecified — omits the header, no `preflight`

`maxAge`: Sets the `Access-Control-Allow-Max-Age` header.

Possible values for `maxAge`

- An integer value in milliseconds for TTL to cache the request
- If unspecified, the request is not cached

`preflightContinue`: Passes the CORS `preflight` response to the next handler.

The default configuration without setting any values allows all origins and methods without `preflight`. Keep in mind that complex CORS requests, other than GET, HEAD, and POST, will fail without `preflight`, so make sure you enable `preflight` in the configuration when using them. Without setting any values, the configuration defaults to:

```
{
    "origin": "*",
    "methods": "GET,HEAD,PUT,PATCH,POST,DELETE",
    "preflightContinue": false
}
```

Code examples for CORS npm

These examples demonstrate the flexibility of CORS npm for specific configurations. Note that the express and cors packages are always required.

Enable CORS globally for all origins and all routes

The simplest implementation of CORS npm enables CORS for all origins and all requests. The following example enables CORS for an arbitrary route, " / product/:id", for a GET request by telling the entire app to use CORS for all routes:

```
var express = require('express')
  , cors = require('cors')
  , app = express();

app.use(cors()); // this tells the app to use CORS for all requests
and all routes

app.get('/product/:id', function(req, res, next){
  res.json({msg: 'CORS is enabled for all origins'});
});

app.listen(80, function(){
  console.log('CORS is enabled on the web server listening on port
80');
});
```

Allowing CORS for dynamic origins for a specific route

The following example uses `corsOptions` to check whether the domain making the request is in the whitelisted array with a `callback` function, which returns null if it doesn't find a match. This CORS option is passed to the route `"product/:id"`, which is the only route that has CORS enabled. The allowed origins can become dynamic by changing the value of the variable `"whitelist"`:

```
var express = require('express')
  , cors = require('cors')
  , app = express();

// define the whitelisted domains and set the CORS options to check
them
var whitelist = ['http://localdomain.com', 'http://localdomain-other.
com'];
var corsOptions = {
  origin: function(origin, callback){
    var originWhitelisted = whitelist.indexOf(origin) !== -1;
    callback(null, originWhitelisted);
  }
};

// add the CORS options to a specific route /product/:id for a GET
request
app.get('/product/:id', cors(corsOptions), function(req, res, next){
  res.json({msg: 'A whitelisted domain matches and CORS is enabled for
route product/:id'});
});

// log that CORS is enabled on the server
app.listen(80, function(){
  console.log(''CORS is enabled on the web server listening on port
80'');
});
```

You may set different CORS options for specific routes, or sets of routes, by defining the options assigned to unique variable names, for example `"corsUserOptions"`. Pass the specific configuration variable to each route that requires that set of options.

Enabling CORS preflight

CORS requests that use an HTTP method other than GET, HEAD, or POST (for example, DELETE), or that use custom headers, are considered complex and require a preflight request before proceeding with the CORS requests. Enable preflight by adding an OPTIONS handler for the route:

```
var express = require('express')
  , cors = require('cors')
  , app = express();

// add the OPTIONS handler
app.options('/products/:id', cors()); // options is added to the route
/products/:id

// use the OPTIONS handler for the DELETE method on the route /
products/:id
app.del('/products/:id', cors(), function(req, res, next){
  res.json({msg: 'CORS is enabled with preflight on the route '/
products/:id' for the DELETE method for all origins!'});
});

app.listen(80, function(){
  console.log('CORS is enabled on the web server listening on port
80'');
});
```

> You can enable preflight globally on all routes with the wildcard:
>
> ```
> app.options('*', cors());
> ```

Configuring CORS asynchronously

One of the reasons we use Node.js frameworks is to take advantage of their asynchronous abilities—handling multiple tasks at the same time. Here, we use a callback function corsDelegateOptions and add it to the CORS parameter passed to the route /products/:id. The callback function can handle multiple requests asynchronously:

```
var express = require('express')
  , cors = require('cors')
  , app = express();
  // define the allowed origins stored in a variable
var whitelist = ['http://example1.com', 'http://example2.com'];
```

```
// create the callback function
var corsDelegateOptions = function(req, callback){
  var corsOptions;
  if(whitelist.indexOf(req.header('Origin')) !== -1){
    corsOptions = { origin: true }; // the requested origin in the
CORS response matches and is allowed
  }else{
    corsOptions = { origin: false }; // the requested origin in the
CORS response doesn't match, and CORS is disabled for this request
  }
  callback(null, corsOptions); // callback expects two parameters:
error and options
};

// add the callback function to the cors parameter for the route /
products/:id for a GET request
app.get('/products/:id', cors(corsDelegateOptions), function(req, res,
next){
  res.json({msg: ''A whitelisted domain matches and CORS is enabled
for route product/:id'});
});

app.listen(80, function(){
  console.log('CORS is enabled on the web server listening on port
80'');
});
```

CORS in AngularJS

AngularJS is designed to be a client-side application, meaning it renders in the client browser and does not run on the server. Therefore, you can't make a CORS request to an AngularJS frontend. CORS in AngularJS creates requests from the application for resources on other domains, typically with GET.

If your AngularJS application is connected to a JavaScript server, then you may be able to use CORS in the server application before sending the data to AngularJS. How you implement CORS depends on the server framework.

Isomorphic JavaScript runs the same codebase on the server and in the client browser. The JavaScript server is typically built with Node.js. In an isomorphic JavaScript application with AngularJS on the frontend, CORS requests are handled by the JavaScript server.

Enabling CORS in AngularJS

To enable CORS in AngularJS, we will create a service, which we will call `appName`. Configure `$httpProvider.defaults` with `useXDomain` so that the cross-domain requests are also compatible with Internet Explorer 9 or earlier:

```
var  appName = angular.module('appName', [
      'appNameApiService']);

appName.config(['$httpProvider', function($httpProvider) {
      $httpProvider.defaults.useXDomain = true;
      $httpProvider.defaults.headers.common['X-Requested-With'];
   }
]);
```

Making a CORS request in AngularJS

You can make a CORS request in AngularJS as an HTTP request, or as a resource request. The following code uses GET as an HTTP request against the target domain, and also returns data about a user with the ID 123 as a resource request. Note that the cross-domain request is enabled and is compatible with Internet Explorer 9 and earlier by setting `$http.defaults.useXDomain` to true in the `corsController`. You can choose your own names for the `ModuleName` and `corsControllerName`:

```
angular.module(''ModuleName'', ['ngResource']).controller('corsControl
lerName', function ($scope, $http, $resource) {
    $http.defaults.useXDomain = true; // support IE <= 9

    // make the GET request
    $scope.useHttp = function() {
        $http.get('http://targetdomain.com')
            .success(function(data) {
                alert(data.ok);
            });
    };

    // make the User resource request
    $scope.useResource = function() {
        var User = $resource('http://targetdomain.com', {
            userId: '@id'
        });
        User.get({
            userId: 123
```

```
    }, function(data) {
        alert(data.ok);
    });
  };
});
```

CORS in Backbone.js

Like AngularJS, Backbone.js relies on a separate server application, typically provided by a Node.js server.

If you want to make a CORS request from a Backbone.js application, you need to modify Backbone.sync, which handles HTTP requests, to add the cross-domain options. You also want to add the `withCredentials` property to Backbone.sync for full access to cookies and other information on the target server that are controlled by the same origin policy.

Backbone.sync uses its own syntax for mapping its names for CRUD operations to REST methods. **CRUD** is an acronym derived from "create", "read", "update", and "delete". Be mindful of the underlying HTTP method when using Backbone.js syntax for methods, and whether the HTTP method requires `preflight` for CORS. Backbone.sync maps its CRUD methods to HTTP methods, as follows:

Backbone.sync Method Name	REST HTTP Method
create	POST /collection
read	GET /collection[/id]
update	PUT /collection/id
patch	PATCH /collection/id
delete	DELETE /collection/id

Using Backbone.CrossDomain to modify Backbone.sync

If you want a quick and easy way to add CORS support to Backbone.js, we recommend using this extension.

`Backbone.CrossDomain` is a project hosted on GitHub that adds CORS support to Backbone.sync for IE 7-9 with the `XDomainRequest` object, and also uses XHR for clients that support it. It can be installed with npm and Bower. It can also be loaded with the **asynchronous module definition (AMD)** API in RequireJS if you are using Backbone.js with the RequireJS module loader.

The GitHub project for `Backbone.CrossDomain` is hosted at .

How to proxy Backbone.sync for cross-domain requests

If you need to configure Backbone.sync yourself without using `Backbone.CrossDomain`, the following code modifies the default Backbone.sync options by adding `options.crossdomain = true` and `options.xhrFields = {withCredentials:true}`.

```
var corsSync= Backbone.sync;
Backbone.sync = function(method, model, options) {
  options || (options = {});

  // make sure crossDomain is enabled in the options
  if (!options.crossDomain) {
    options.crossDomain = true;
  }

  // make sure that options.xhrFields is set with
withCredentials:true
  if (!options.xhrFields) {
    options.xhrFields = {withCredentials:true};
  }
  return corsSync(method, model, options);
};
```

jQuery Ajax needs to use the XHR Header

Backbone.js is often used together with jQuery. If you have changed the default jQuery header `X-Requested-With: XMLHttpRequest`, which is needed for CORS in JavaScript, then CORS requests made with jQuery can fail. You can use `$.ajaxSetup` to set the necessary header:

```
$.ajaxSetup({
    headers: { 'X-Requested-With' : 'XMLHttpRequest' }
});
```

Ember.js also relies on CORS-enabled jQuery AJAX

Whether using Ember.js alone, with Ember data modeling, or with ROR Rack, the key is to configure jQuery AJAX for CORS. In this example, both `crossDomain` and `withCredentials` are enabled:

```
$.ajaxSetup({
  crossDomain: true,
  xhrFields: {
    withCredentials: true
  }
});
```

Socket.IO manages origins for security

Similar to the CORS concept of allowing requests to "bend" the same origin policy, `Socket.IO` manages the allowed origins for security. The allowed origin(s) need to be explicitly set. In this code snippet from `Socket.IO` core, we can see how it parses the origin to match an allowed pattern of protocol, host name, and port:

```
var origin = request.headers.origin || request.headers.referer
  , origins = this.get('origins');

var parts = url.parse(origin);
parts.port = parts.port || 80;
var ok =
  ~origins.indexOf(parts.hostname + ':' + parts.port) ||
  ~origins.indexOf(parts.hostname + ':*') ||
  ~origins.indexOf('*:' + parts.port);
```

Define the allowed origin(s) with the protocol, host name, and port in the server portion of the require statement. In the following example, three origin domains are permitted. Note that each includes all three parts. The wildcard * can be used to allow any port number, or the port number can be specified:

```
var io = require('socket.io')(server, {origins:'https://localdomain1.
com:* http://localdomain2.dom:8080  http://www.localdomain3.com:*'});
```

Node.js and JavaScript frameworks are evolving rapidly

We covered some of the techniques used to allow cross-origin requests in some of the popular JavaScript frameworks.

These frameworks are evolving rapidly, and new techniques are sure to be developed between the time of writing and when you read this section. Always read your project documentation for the latest information.

You may also create your own methods with your knowledge of the CORS specification, since JavaScript is a loosely-structured language.

Summary

We have learned some important ways of applying CORS in Node.js. Let us have a quick recap of what we have learned.

Node.js provides a web server built with JavaScript, and can be combined with many other JS frameworks as the application server.

Although some frameworks have specific syntax for implementing CORS, they all follow the CORS specification by specifying the allowed origin(s) and method(s). More robust frameworks allow custom headers, such as `Content-Type` and `preflight`, when required for complex CORS requests.

JavaScript frameworks may depend on the jQuery `XHR` object, which must be configured properly to allow cross-origin requests.

JavaScript frameworks are evolving rapidly. The examples here may become outdated. Always refer to the project documentation for up-to-date information.

With knowledge of the CORS specification, you may create your own techniques using JavaScript based on these examples, depending on the specific needs of your application.

Now you know most of the techniques in enabling CORS across various platforms. In the next chapter, we will learn about the best practices the industry recommends when enabling CORS.

References

https://en.wikipedia.org/wiki/Node.js

https://en.wikipedia.org/wiki/Node.js

8

CORS Best Practices

We have learned a lot about implementing CORS on various platforms. Now we will look at the best practices in applying CORS.

In this chapter, we will learn about the following:

- Enabling API to public CORS requests
- Limiting API to allow CORS requests to a whitelisted set of origins
- Protecting against CSRF (cross-site request forgery)
- Minimizing preflight requests

Enabling API to public CORS requests

As we know, CORS allows restricted access to resources from another domain (for example, fonts, images, and so on). Generally, it is a browser's responsibility to honor the restriction by verifying the headers in the request and the responses from the client and the server.

There are a few resources that we may request from our domain to any external domains. Fonts and images are a few such example resources. To allow such resources to be served, we need to enable the APIs to serve resources to any public CORS requests.

As we discussed earlier, we need to add a wildcard (*) to the `Access-Control-Allow-Origin` header in the response header from the server. A wildcard same-origin policy is suitable when an API response content is meant to consume publicly and is intended to be accessed by anyone on the Internet. A wildcard (*) does not allow any request to supply credentials or cookies.

Limiting API to allow CORS requests to a whitelisted set of origins

In the previous section, we discussed allowing all the origins to access the resources available from different origins. We only need to enable such options if the resource needs to be served publicly to any domain from the API service. Otherwise, it is good practice to allow CORS requests only to the whitelisted set of origins. This can be achieved by replacing the wildcard (*) and adding the specific set of origins that are allowed to access the resources from the API.

Protecting against cross-site request forgery (CSRF)

A CSRF attack is a malicious action that involves sending a request to any website that is already authenticated by the user. This way, it enables the attacker to perform any functionality in the target website via the browser of the user.

The best practice to prevent **cross-site request forgery (CSRF)** is to append unpredictable challenge tokens to requests and associate them with the user sessions. The unpredictable challenge tokens should be unique per user session or per request. These unpredictable challenge tokens should be verified to make sure the request is valid and is coming from a valid source. If the unpredictable challenge token is not valid, then the request is coming from a source other than the user, and that needs to be blocked.

Minimizing preflight requests

Preflight requests are sent by browsers in order to make sure that the actual requests are trusted by the servers. It means that the server will respond with the details in the header if the method, origin, and headers being sent on the request are safe to process. This is required if and when you are making requests across different origins.

Preflight requests will be triggered by a browser if the content-type in a request is of type JSON. Using the preflight cache, you can reduce the number of preflight requests. The preflight is cached and maintained by origin or URL, so each URL or origin will have its own preflight cached in the browser. Preflight helps avoid the preflight performance hit.

Configuring the API to return only the simple content-types, such as `application/x-www-form-urlencoded`, `multipart/form-data` or `text/plain`, in the accepted header will avoid preflight requests. Moving the variables to a query string from the URL path increases the ratio of preflight caching and minimizes the preflight requests.

Summary

That's all, folks! You have learned the important elements of securing a web application using cross-site resource sharing.

In this chapter, we discussed some of the best practices in applying CORS.

We started by talking about enabling the API to accept public CORS requests. Then we discussed the limiting of API to allow CORS requests to a whitelisted set of origins.

Later, we discussed the best practices in protecting against **cross-site request forgery (CSRF)**.

Finally, we saw the various options for minimizing the preflight requests from browsers to servers.

Now you know every aspect of applying CORS, and you can be very confident about suggesting various techniques and best practices in handling cross-site resource sharing.

Index

B

Backbone.CrossDomain
 URL 114
 used, for modifying Backbone.sync 113
Backbone.js
 about 104
 Ember.js, relying on CORS-enabled jQuery
  AJAX 115
 origins, managing with Socket.IO for
  security 115
 with CORS 113
 XHR Header, using with jQuery Ajax 114
Backbone.sync
 modifying, with
  Backbone.CrossDomain 113
 proxying, for cross-domain requests 114
Box API 97

C

Can I Use
 URL 77
Chrome
 preflight, issues 16
cloud APIs
 CORS requests 79, 80
com.adobe.cq.social.commons.cors package
 CORSAuthenticationFilter class,
  methods 58
 CORSAuthInfoPostProcessor class,
  methods 58
 CORSConfig class, methods 58
Connect.js 103
Content Delivery Network (CDN) 54
cookies 2, 13
cors-anywhere package
 about 29
 URL 29
CorsMessageHandler
 enabling 66
CORS npm
 code examples 108
 Connect.js middleware, using for
  Express.js 106

CORS npm, configuration options
 allowedHeaders 106
 credentials 107
 exposedHeaders 107
 maxAge 107
 methods 106
 origin 106
 preflightContinue 107
CORS requests
 incoming 43, 44, 64
CORS rules
 reference 95
CORS usability
 about 31, 32
 AJAX support, detecting in browser 33
 browser support 32, 33
 HTTP request headers 36
 HTTP response headers 36, 37
 preflight, using for non-simple CORS
  requests 34, 35
CORS XML-RPC plugin
 URL 50
Cross Origin Resource Sharing (CORS)
 about 5
 allowing 3
 and WebSocket 23
 authenticated access, to Google APIs 88
 debugging 18
 DOM elements, allowing 4
 DOM elements, distributing to multiple
  domains 10-12
 enabling, in Drupal with custom code 50
 enabling, with server configuration 20
 example 6-9
 in Amazon Simple Storage Service
  (Amazon S3) 80
 implementing, in Drupal 50
 in Box API 97
 in Dropbox API 98
 in Google Cloud Storage 84
 in IBM Cloudant 91
 in WebSocket 4
 in WordPress 44
 in Windows Azure Storage 93
 jQuery, using 18
 jQuery CORS AJAX plugin 20
 limited access 4

request methods 14
SAAS WordPress.com, support for 44, 45
security, adding for whitelisted domains 13
troubleshooting 18
used, in self-hosted WordPress 47
via jQuery 15
whitelisted domains, securing 12
with preflight 14
cross-site request forgery (CSRF)
about 118
preflight requests, minimizing 118
protecting against 118
Cross-Site WebSocket Hijacking (CSWSH) 23
CRUD 113

D

Dropbox API
about 98
reference 99
Dropbox chooser
URL 98
Drupal
contributed modules, supporting CORS 51
CORS, enabling with custom code 50
CORS headers, adding with custom code 51
CORS, implementing 50
CORS module 52-54
CORS support, adding with .htaccess 51
Drupal 8 core, supporting CORS 55
drupal_add_http_header function, using 50
Drupal Amazon S3 CORS upload module
about 54
URL 54
Drupal CDN module
about 54
URL 54
dynamic ASP.NET Web API CORS policies
about 72
custom CORS policy attribute classes 72
custom CORS policy class 72
custom CORS policy provider factory 74
custom policy provider factory 73
DynamicPolicyProviderFactory, registering in WebApiConfig 74

E

Edge 78
Ember.js
relying, on CORS-enabled jQuery AJAX 115
EnableCorsAttribute class
CORS policies, setting 67
EnableCors class attributes
CORS, disallowing in classes 70
CORS, disallowing in methods 70
CORS policy, setting with wildcards 69
DisableCors attribute, using 71
explicit values, using for HTTP methods 70
global CORS policy, setting with WebApiConfig class 70
Enterprise Service Bus (ESB) 26
examples, CORS npm
CORS, allowing for dynamic origins for specific route 109
CORS, configuring asynchronously 110
CORS, enabling for all origins 108
CORS, enabling for all routes 108
CORS preflight, enabling 110
Express.js
about 103
Connect.js middleware, using with CORS npm 106
with CORS 105

F

Firefox
preflight, issues 16

G

Google API Client Library
URL 88
Google APIs
authenticated access, with CORS 88
authenticated CORS requests, creating with OAuth 90
CORS request 89
Google API client library, adding for JavaScript 89
Google API keys 88
URL 89

Google App Engine
  proxy server, creating 27
  URL 27
Google Cloud Storage
  cached preflight request problems,
        troubleshooting 87
  CORS, configuring on bucket 84
  CORS-related problems,
        troubleshooting 86
  CORS, using 84
  gsutil cors set, using 85
  headers problems, troubleshooting 87
  resumable upload protocol problems,
        troubleshooting 88
  XML API, using 85
Google Drive SDK
  reference 91

H

Heroku
  URL 29
HTML5 Web Messaging
  reference 23
HTTP_ORIGIN header
  inspecting 38

I

IBM Cloudant
  about 91
  CORS configuration, modifying 91, 92
  CORS configuration, obtaining 91
  security considerations 92
Internet Explorer
  about 78
  preflight, issues 16
Internet Explorer exception policy 3
Internet Information Service (IIS)
        manager 65

J

JavaScript frameworks
  AngularJS 103
  Backbone.js 104
  Connect.js 103
  Ember.js 104

  evolving 116
  Express.js 103
  popularity 102
  ReactJS 104
  Socket.IO 104
  with Node.js 103
Joomla
  CORS, allowing in .htaccess file 55
  CORS, enabling in 55
  matware-libraries, on GitHub 55
  setHeader, in JApplication web 55
jQuery
  Cross Origin Resource Sharing (CORS),
        using 18
  using 15
jQuery Ajax
  XHR Header, using 114
jQuery CORS AJAX plugin
  about 20
  URL 20
JSON-P
  about 21
  example 21
  limitations 21
  risks 21
  URL 22
  validation standard 22

L

Local Domain 6
local network firewall
  proxy, using 27

M

matware-libraries
  on GitHub 55
  URL 55
model-view-controller (MVC) 103, 104
model-view-presenter (MVP) 104
model-view-viewmodel (MVVM) 103
mod_proxy
  URL 28

JavaScript permissions, requiring 5
reference 1
security
access, limiting with wildcard
Access-Control-Allow-Origin 38
enhancing 38
Open Web Application Security Project
(OWASP) 41
self-hosted WordPress
Access-Control-Allow-Origin header,
adding in template 48
CORS, using 47
WordPress plugins, for CORS 48
setHeader
in JApplication web 55
Shared Access Signature (SAS) 93
Simple Object Access Protocol (SOAP) 49
Socket.IO
about 22, 104
origins, managing for security 115
URL 22
Software As A Service (SAAS) 44

T

Target Domain 6
token
URL, for validation 47
validating, for security 46
token request endpoints
URL 45

U

unauthenticated GET requests
to WordPress.com 45
user access token
obtaining 46
storing 46

W

web.config
CORS headers, setting globally for IIS7
Server 64

WebSocket
about 22
Cross Origin Resource Sharing (CORS) 4
handshakes 23
reference 22
risks 23
whitelist
in application manager 46
wildcard Access-Control-Allow-Origin
access, limiting 38
HTTP_ORIGIN header, inspecting 38
requesting, with credentials 39-41
window.postMessage method
about 23
risks 24
security measures 24
Windows Azure Storage
about 93
code examples 94
CORS, configuring dynamically 95
CORS, enabling for blob (file) service 95
CORS, for table service 97
CORS, for Windows Azure Blobs 93
CORS, for Windows Azure Table 93
CORS, usage scenarios 93
image, uploading with CORS in
ASP.NET 96
preflight requests 94
reference 93
static CORS rules 94, 95
**Windows Communication Foundation
(WCF) 77**
Windows IIS Server
Access-Control-Allow-Origin header,
setting globally 64
CORS headers, setting globally for
IIS 8.5 65
WordPress
authenticated requests, creating 45
CORS 44
unauthenticated GET requests 45
URL, for REST API 46
WordPress plugins
CORS XML-RPC plugin, allowing 49, 50
for CORS 48
WP-CORS plugin 48

World Wide Web 25
World Wide Web Consortium (W3C)
  URL 5
WP-CORS plugin
  about 48
  URL 49

X

XML API
  CORS configuration, modifying on
      bucket 86
  CORS configuration, obtaining for
      bucket 86
  using, in Google Cloud Storage 85
XMLHttpRequest (XHR) 2, 5
XML-RPC
  URL 49